"When You Know."
xxx

When You Know

Kiki Archer

Title: When You Know
ID: 14566958
ISBN: 978-1-291-82118-5

K.A Books *Publishers*

www.kikiarcher.com

Twitter: @kikiarcherbooks

Published by K.A Books 2014

Editor: Jayne Fereday

Author photograph: **Ian France** www.ianfrance.com

ISBN: 978-1-291-82118-5

CHAPTER ONE

"There's a fine line between perception and paranoia."

Susan frowned. "Who said that?"

Jenna nodded. "I did."

"No, I mean, where's the quote from?"

Jenna puffed up proudly and smiled. "Actually, it's mine. I invented it and I even googled it once to make sure no one's said it before."

Susan laughed. "I'm sure someone's said it before."

"No, they haven't. It's mine and I'm claiming it, and I think it perfectly sums up what we're about to go through."

Susan lifted her head and looked around the busy airport terminal. "Departures?"

"No!" said Jenna. "I'm talking about *your* perception versus *your* paranoia. You're paranoid that I'm going to run off with some ski girl, or barmaid, or chairlift operator—"

"Or Amber," added Susan, only half joking.

Jenna shook her head and shunted her holdall forwards with her feet, moving fractionally closer to the busy check-in desk, aware that their queue had to snake around another four corners before they got anywhere near the front. "See, you're paranoid I'm going to start something with Amber again." She paused. "And I understand why. Your paranoia's based on your perception that I sleep around."

"It's not a perception Jenna, it's a fact, and I'm not trying to be mean here, and I'm actually not worried you'll sleep around, but you two have history. I'm worried you'll sleep with her. Amber wants you, and not so long ago you wanted her too." Susan took a sharp intake of breath. "Against the bar, on the bar, between her legs—"

Jenna pressed her finger onto Susan's lips. "Shhh. Susan, please, just shhh. You're the one I love. You're the one I want. You're the one I can't stop thinking about. You're the one who's given me the most memorable week ever." She smiled. "I'm one hundred percent sure of everything."

1

Susan looked into Jenna's deep brown eyes and sighed. "I want to believe you, trust me I do—" The finger was back, but Susan continued to talk. "I'm just a realist—"

"Sorry, no, you're muffled, I can't hear you." Jenna raised her eyebrows. "If I remove this finger will you listen? Just listen?"

Susan noticed the gap in the queue that had appeared in front of them. "Fine," she said, sucking her lips and bringing them back to life. "We need to move forwards anyway."

Jenna stayed still. "You're the love of my life, and I'm not going anywhere."

Susan bent down and took hold of the bag, pushing it forwards. "Yes you are. You're going to Morzine, for the next three months."

Jenna stepped in front of Susan and took hold of her shoulders. "Yes, to finish the season. My last season." She shook her gently. "I'm choosing you, Susan. I'm choosing us."

Susan pulled her left arm free and checked her watch. She exhaled heavily and looked around at the crowded queue of holiday makers. Most were already wearing their big ski jackets and padded Moon Boots, eagerly anticipating their time in the snow. "You'll be gone for three months. She'll be there, as will all of your other lady-loving ski reps. I won't."

"Paranoia, paranoia, paranoia…"

"Maybe you're right. But it's not paranoia. I'm just worried. It's a tiny niggling doubt in the back of my mind based on the things I've seen and the things you've told me."

"There's a fine line between perception and paranoia."

"Yes, I get it, great quote."

Jenna grinned. "I'm teasing you, Susan. I've changed. You've changed me. There's no way I'd ever jeopardise what we've got."

Susan took another small step forwards and waited for the latest loud echoing airport announcement to stop. She checked her watch once more. "And what *have* we got?"

Jenna frowned. "We've got a blossoming relationship. We've got a shared desire to make this work." She paused. "We've got love … haven't we?"

Susan sighed. "It's been two weeks in total. Maybe this whirlwind's blinded us. Maybe we should just use this time to step back from the whole situation and try and figure out what's going on. Maybe—"

"Whoa, whoa, whoa." Jenna shook her head. "Stop. Where's this coming from?"

Susan was about to reply when she felt a sharp bang on the back of her heel. "Oww," she gasped, looking down and realising the noisy family from behind had once again slid their skis too far forwards in the queue.

"Sorry," said the man, stepping over his family's mound of luggage and bending down to retrieve the long bag. He stood back up, totally hot and bothered, all trussed up in his ski suit and hat. "Bloody check-in always takes too long. The wife told me to travel in my ski gear. She said there wasn't enough room in the suitcase for all this padded stuff." He looked down at Jenna's small piece of hand luggage. "Morzine?" he asked with a frown.

Jenna nodded. "I'm a ski rep. I've had a week off. I'm flying back out to finish the season."

The man stepped in closer, desperate for a break from his over excitable children and constantly complaining wife. "Sisters?"

"Yes," said Susan.

"No," said Jenna, at exactly the same time.

Jenna looked at Susan and frowned. "You're my girlfriend."

Susan blushed. "Sorry, I wasn't thinking." She coughed and lowered her voice. "But we don't really need to announce it over the Tannoy, do we?"

"Girlfriends, eh? You're brave, love," said the man, directing his attention to Susan, "letting her loose on the slopes. Haven't you seen that programme, *Snow, Sex, and Suspicious Parents*? It's always the ski reps who end up getting off with those young kids." He grinned at Jenna. "But hey, what happens on the slopes stays on the slopes, right?" He nodded his head backwards. "I used to have a real life before my wife came along and put a dampener on things."

Jenna couldn't avoid focusing on his perspiring red cheeks. "It's my last season. I'm moving back in April and I'm re-training as a teacher."

"If you get accepted," added Susan.

"What? What is this?" asked Jenna, completely confused.

"CARL!" The shout was loud. "Would you PLEASE get the passports out? We are NEARLY at the FRONT of the queue."

The man looked at Susan and Jenna and rolled his eyes. "She always does this. Makes me stand in this bloody queue, with my bloody ski stuff on, holding all of the bloody documents, well before we even reach the bloody check-in desk."

"CARL! It's moving! Would you PLEASE get the documents out? AND the passports. AND we reserved our seats so you'll need that evidence too. Jackie's having a meal on the plane, and she's asked for the vegetarian dish so we'll need to show them the paperwork for that as well."

The man lifted his woolly hat and wiped his forehead. "Yes, darling," he said, forcing his smile as he flared his nostrils.

Jenna watched him clamber back over the piles of luggage before turning to Susan and shaking her head. "Sisters?"

"We don't need to tell strangers our business."

"We're a couple, Susan. I'm proud to call you mine."

Susan pushed Jenna's bag with the inside of her foot, rounding the final corner. "I don't want to force you into anything."

"Hey! I flew over here, of my own accord, to give you that ridiculously expensive thimble for your really rather cute thimble collection, because I love you."

Susan shrugged. "It's been two weeks."

"Yes, and when you know, you know."

"I know you've got three months of temptation ahead of you."

Jenna shook her head. "Susan, what is this? Should I take offence, or are *you* having doubts?"

"I'm just trying to be realistic."

"Why haven't you mentioned this before? Why leave it to the last minute?" Jenna dropped her eyes to her holdall. "Fine, you go off and play the field. Let's see where we're at when I get back."

"Is that what you want?"

"No!" said Jenna. "But it's sounding like you do!" She looked at the group of young men who were being called to check-in, obviously off on some sort of skiing stag do, and already rather merry. "We're checking-in next and we've still got some time for a coffee. We need to get this sorted, Susan. We need to know the rules."

"So you do want flexibility then? You do want your final few months of freedom?"

Jenna shook her head even harder. "No, Susan! I want you!"

"NEXT." The shout was high pitched and official.

Jenna picked up her hand luggage, feeling incredibly flustered, wondering where on earth Susan's outburst had come from. She tried to smile at the dolled-up check-in lady, but failed. "I've only got one piece of hand luggage," she said with distraction.

"Flying to Morzine?"

Jenna took her eyes off Susan and nodded. "Yes."

The lady looked at both women. "Flying alone?"

"Yes." Jenna reached into her jacket pocket for her documents.

"Did you pack your own bag?"

"Yes," nodded Jenna, handing over her passport.

"Would you like me to check the weight of your hand luggage?"

"No, it's fine. I only flew over last week."

"We have a strict weight restriction of five kilograms for hand luggage."

"It's fine, I always use this bag."

"You haven't bought anything, or added to your luggage while you've been over here?"

"No."

The lady handed Jenna's documents back to her and pressed the button to print out the boarding card. "Departures to the left."

Susan angled her body away from the check-in lady and widened her eyes at Jenna. "The *things*," she mouthed.

Jenna frowned and mouthed back. "What?"

Susan whispered. "In your bag. The things we bought. Maybe you should get it weighed. You don't want them opening your bag at departures."

The check-in lady tore the boarding card from the printer but didn't hand it over. "Everything okay?"

"Yes," said Jenna, suddenly catching on. "Actually, I'd like you to weigh my bag please."

"Did you pack it yourself?" asked the lady staring at Jenna, then Susan, then back at Jenna again.

"Yes," nodded Jenna, lifting it onto the belt.

The lady pressed a button and tapped a long nail on the top of the digital screen which was flickering between 5.0 and 5.1. "You're point one of a kilogram over."

"Hardly," said Jenna, watching the numbers come to a final standstill. "It'll be okay, won't it?"

The lady pursed her red lips. "We have a strict five kilogram limit on hand luggage. There's a forty pound charge if you want to increase your allowance." She tapped the screen again. "Five point one."

"What? That's outrageous."

"Company policy."

"My ticket didn't cost much more than that."

"Exactly," announced the lady with authority. "The airline has a right to recoup its generosity."

Susan stepped in. "It's fine. Let's go for a coffee and we'll sort through your bag. I'll keep hold of some things if necessary."

"No, I need everything. I only brought the bare essentials with me."

Susan widened her eyes again. "I'm sure there are a couple of *things* I can take."

"Did you pack your own bag, Madam?" asked the lady once more.

"Yes, it's fine. I'll get it sorted before I go through to departures."

The lady spoke haughtily. "You'll only get sent back here, to the back of this queue, to purchase additional allowance. Is there anything in your luggage I need to know about?" She looked Susan up and down. "Has this lady asked you to carry something on board? Do I need to call security?"

"No! Of course not."

"Would you mind opening your bag for me please, Madam?"

"No, it's fine, we'll sort it out."

"Madam, open your bag please."

"Fine," said Jenna, unzipping the worn holdall. She rummaged around and pulled out two items. "Susan, could you hold these please?"

Susan gasped as the two different shaped dildos were thrust into her hands. "Jenna!"

"There," said Jenna, watching the numbers flash on the screen. She glanced momentarily to the left where the sweaty man from the queue was on his hands and knees at the check-in desk, shifting items of clothing between two open suitcases. Jenna ignored the temptation to listen to his wife's latest lambasting, and turned to the screen instead. "Under five kilograms," she announced with pride. "Departures to the left, you say?"

The check-in lady was open mouthed.

"Thank you for your assistance," added Jenna, zipping the bag back up. "I'll just carry these on." She took the dildos from Susan's shaking hands and thrust one in her left jacket pocket and one in her right, leaving the ends poking out like two cocks in a brothel. "Coffee?" she said, with a nod of her head.

Susan stumbled after her, unable to form her words properly. "T-T-The blue one," she said, eyes fixed on the action. "It's, it's on."

Jenna kept her pace brisk and her head high, ignoring the party in her pocket. "Just walk, Susan, just walk."

CHAPTER TWO

Susan shook her head. "You cannot possibly board the plane with two dildos sticking out of your jacket pocket."

"Why not?" asked Jenna, taking a tentative sip of the creamy mocha. "It's no different to carrying on an iPad, or having a kid's plastic toy in your pocket."

"Because you look like John Wayne with two pistols ready for the draw. Honestly, Jenna, you walked up to that coffee counter like a cowboy entering a saloon."

"They don't bend. It's not like I can double them over." Jenna pushed Susan's hot chocolate across the table. "Don't let it get cold."

Susan left the cup where it was. "Please, we've only got ten minutes. I don't want you carrying them onto the plane."

"Why not?"

Susan blushed. "You know why. They've been—"

"Everywhere!" Jenna started to smile. "That's why I'm taking them with me. I want to remember this crazy, sex-filled week of ours."

"And you need to board the plane with those things to remember?" Susan lifted her eyes to the large departures screen. "Please, Jenna, they'll be calling your gate soon and you're not even past security."

"Fine," sighed Jenna, drawing the two dildos from her pockets and plonking them onto the table. "You take them." She smiled cheekily. "On one condition."

Susan threw her arms on top of the toys. "Are you deliberately trying to embarrass me?"

"The condition is, I want to see them at least twice a week via Skype."

Susan swept the toys onto her lap, coughing as she tried to disguise the squeaking noise of the rubber as it moved across the metal table. "What am I meant to do with them?"

"You're pretty confident already if my memory serves me correctly."

"Jenna! I'm talking about now. My bag's too small and my pockets are tiny."

"Shove them under your jumper, walk to your car and put them in your glove box. When you get back to school nip into your apartment and get a carrier bag or something." Jenna grinned. "Then tonight, when we Skype, you get them out and show me what I'm missing."

"I knew we shouldn't have bought them."

"Bought them or brought them here?"

"Both!"

Jenna lifted the discarded plastic mocha lid from the table and pushed it back onto her cup. "You said we could sex-Skype and FaceTime-fuck every other evening."

"Is this all we have? Is this all we're about? Sex? Just sex?"

Jenna frowned. "What? Why are you saying this?"

Susan pulled herself further under the table, hiding the weight on her lap. "We haven't spent a single minute this week talking about the rules, and now we only have seconds before you disappear for three months."

Jenna reached across the table and took hold of Susan's hands. "We haven't needed to talk about any rules. We're both on the same page. We love each other. We've found that magical thing that everyone always talks about. We've found true love. We've found real love. We've found the kind of love that catches you off guard and sends a crazy, warm, excited buzz straight to your heart when you're least expecting it. We've found the person we want to commit to. The person we want to build a future with." Jenna paused. "We haven't spoken about it because we don't need to speak about it. We feel it, Susan, and feelings always hold so much more power than words. I mean, listen to me waffling on. I can't do justice to what I feel with words alone. It's in my eyes, it's in my heart, it's on my lips, it's at the tips of my fingers as I hold your hands. It's love, Susan, and I've never felt anything as strongly or as passionately before."

Susan pulled her hands away from Jenna's and looked at the floor. "I'm talking practicalities."

"What?" Jenna bent her head and tried to connect with Susan's eyes. "What do you mean? I've observed lessons this week. I've sent in my School Direct training application. I've written to Club Ski telling them it's my final season." She frowned. "How much more practical do you want me to get? Should I put a deposit on a house?" Jenna shook her head. "I don't really want to do that as I'm hoping I can live on the school site like you. But I will if you want me to." She paused again. "Do you want me to fly back every other weekend? Tell me what I need to do, Susan? I thought you understood. I'm in this for the long haul."

Susan lifted her head and nodded at the latest echoing announcement. "That's your flight and you're not even through departures."

"I don't care. I'm not going anywhere until we've got this sorted." Jenna moved her chair around to Susan's side of the table. "What's going on? You were strange in the queue, and you're being even stranger now."

Susan sniffed and wiped a small tear from her cheek. "It's just too good to be true." She lifted her eyes to Jenna's and shook her head. "*You're* too good to be true."

"Susan! I'm not! I'm here! We're here! We have each other! We have love!"

"But I don't want to hold you back."

Jenna threw her arm around Susan's shoulder. "Susan, I've grown into the woman I want to be with you. You've not held me back. You've shown me the light. The possibilities." She smiled. "You've shown me the future, and I can't wait to travel the rest of time with you."

Susan sniffed back a giggle. "Maybe you're right. Maybe you're not the best with words."

"Let me show you then," said Jenna, leaning forwards and planting a small delicate kiss on Susan's lips. "This is love. You feel it, right?"

Susan let out a soft moan. "I feel it."

"So trust me. Believe I feel it too."

Susan pulled away and shook her head. "But practicalities. I'm talking practicalities."

"I don't know what you mean!" gasped Jenna, quickly checking her watch.

"You should go. Please, we'll talk later. I'm just being silly. Ignore me."

"I'm not ignoring any of this. You need to tell me what you're feeling."

Susan took a deep breath. "I'll never force you to be faithful, Jenna. We're apart for three months and I don't expect you to spend that time living like a nun. We're two weeks into a brand new relationship, a relationship neither of us expected, and I guess I just want you to be sure. Really sure. I don't want you getting tempted over there and cursing me for being that dreadful ball and chain around your ankle. I'd rather you had your final few months of freedom and then when you're back over here we pick up properly, like a proper couple who see each other on a daily basis."

"Why? Why would you want that?"

"Because I love you."

Jenna smiled and shook her head. "You really are one lovable dafty, Susan Quinn."

"And you're one sex-crazed, Hollywood hottie, Jenna James. There's no way I'll be able to satisfy your needs from a thousand miles away."

"Hmm, I think you might surprise yourself. We've got Skype, FaceTime, Snapchat, Dingtone—"

"But we haven't got each other."

"Yes we have, Susan!" Jenna reached out and placed her hand on Susan's heart. "In here. We're connected. I know you feel it, because I feel you feeling it too, and we're going to be fine. We're going to be just fine. Now kiss me like you mean it."

Susan closed her eyes, oblivious to the hubbub around her, and lost herself in Jenna's love. "Thank you," she said, finally pulling away. "Thank you for being you."

Jenna coughed and sucked on her lips. "Wow, you're certainly getting better at these public displays of affection." She stood up and lifted her arms to the sides. "And see, no one's even paying us the slightest bit of attention."

"I'm trying," said Susan, rising from her seat. "It's a confidence thing I guess." Susan gasped as the two dildos rolled off her lap and bounced under the table, stopping in front of the coffee shop's counter.

Jenna dived to the floor and grabbed them as casually as she could. "My darling," she whispered, standing back up and passing them to Susan, "they must have dropped out."

"Stop it," said Susan, thrusting them under her jumper. "I'm proud of my pelvic floor."

"Show me on Snapchat?"

"You know I have no idea what that is."

Jenna bent down and lifted her holdall. "You'll have fun finding out then," she said, smiling. "Right. I'm running. Literally running."

Susan kept hold of the bulge under her jumper and stepped forwards, gently kissing Jenna on the lips. "I love you."

"And I love you too. We'll be fine. Trust me." Jenna slung her arm around Susan's shoulder one final time. "You're my one, Susan, and nothing and no one will ever change that."

"Run," said Susan, nodding towards departures.

"I'm running," said Jenna, dashing back in for one final hug. "Are there two dildos under your jumper or are you just pleased to see me?"

"Go, you crazy lady!" ordered Susan.

"Going," shouted Jenna, almost falling over herself as she ran towards departures. "We'll be fine, trust me."

"I do," whispered Susan, gently nodding her head.

CHAPTER THREE

Susan eased her foot off the accelerator and gently tapped the padded indicator, admiring once again how smoothly her Prius Hybrid slowed without any need for a clunky gear change or clumsy pedal action. The car had been her biggest purchase to date and she was proud of its eco-friendly, low emission rating. Not to mention the fact it did sixty miles to the gallon. A far cry from her old Suzuki Vitara passed down to her from her great aunt almost nine years ago. The boxy jeep barely got up the school drive without needing a refuel. Plus she always felt she looked like a hairdresser or drug dealer driving the thing and had been desperate to save up for a real teacher's car from the moment she'd started working at St Wilfred's, pleased that, after five years, she now finally looked the part.

Susan drove past the large stone sign that stood proud on the grassy mound, announcing the entrance to St Wilfred's All-Girls School, est. 1854. The drive up to the imposing red-brick building wound the long way around the grounds, no doubt intended to make potential parents marvel at the vast expanse of school owned land. An idyllic yet stately setting for their daughters' education. There were currently 550 girls at the school. Seventy five percent were boarders, and the rest were day girls. Susan Quinn knew them all by name, as did the fifty nine other members of staff. St Wilf's was like that. Homely.

Susan sighed to herself. Her life was good: she enjoyed her job, she had a supportive family, her colleagues seemed to like her, and now, now she had someone special. She glanced down at the futuristic clock on the minimalistic dashboard, smiling to herself at the vision of Jenna crashing through the doors to departures.

Susan rounded a bend and noticed Bob the groundsman smiling and waving his trowel. She gently applied the brake and opened the window, gasping as the cold February air caught her off guard. "Hey, Bob," she shouted. "It's a bit cold for planting today, isn't it?"

Bob stretched out the trowel to the large patch of soil behind him. "If I don't get these bulbs in today we won't see the school crest come spring."

"This one's always the best floral display," said Susan with a smile.

"That it is. That it is."

"Can I get someone to send you down a flask of something warm?"

Bob bent down and jammed his trowel into the soil. "Actually," he said, shuffling down the small verge, "you could give me some good news."

Susan opened her window even wider and smiled at the fresh peat smell that Bob brought with him. "What's that then?"

"Tell me that lovely lady friend of yours, Madam James, tell me she's got the job." Bob leaned further into the window and adjusted his flat cap. "Every day, every day I tell you, she came out to find me. Asked what I was planting. A real charmer she is. She'd be a wonderful addition to the school, and I'm thinking I should express my opinion to the new principal. Jenna said she'd like to get involved with the patterns for the floral displays. Told me she never understood how you could make pictures and words with flowers." Bob laughed. "Was asking me how I knew which colour bulbs were which." Bob nodded. "A great addition. A great addition I tell you. I told her she'd have to come back in the summer to see the grounds in all their glory. I do hope she gets the job. Truly I do." He smiled. "Been nice to see you beaming too, Madam Quinn."

"Oh, Bob, it's Susan, and she's Jenna, and there's no job. She just wants to do her SDTP here."

Bob scratched his grey sideburns. "Speak English to me. You know I hate the jargon."

Susan discreetly turned up the heating, trying to counteract the cold air streaming into her car. "Her School Direct Training Programme. It's a fast track scheme for experienced graduates. She'd get paid to train on site, in the classroom, and at the end of the year she'd have her NQT status."

Bob rolled his eyes.

"She'd be a Newly Qualified Teacher. I guess then she'd have to ask if there was a full-time position available."

"There's always a job for family."

"Bob, she's not family."

"She might be soon though, hey. She might be soon." He grinned. "Ladies like you can marry in March."

"I'll bear that in mind, Bob," said Susan, smiling.

"Or you can civil partner her right now if you want. But I'd hang on for the full shebang. You could have the reception in the Great Hall. We may be an ancient establishment, but we certainly do move with the times." He chuckled to himself. "They even got one of the receptionists to type up all of my planting notes and display designs. Covered in soil, those things were. Covered in soil I tell you. Safe on some computer now though." He nodded. "But I mean it, Madam Quinn, she's a lovely lady, a lovely lady."

Susan blew warm air onto her hands. "I'm glad you approve, Bob. Are you sure I can't get someone to send down a flask?"

"Of course I approve. She's a keeper that Madam James, a real keeper." Bob pulled himself upright and nodded towards his large gardener's trolley. "I'm sorted. Thank you though. You have a good day, Madam Quinn. You have a good day."

Susan waited for Bob to turn away before closing her window and increasing the heat once more.

"Damn pesky weather! It's colder here than in Morzine!" Marcus Ramsbottom had opened the passenger door of the Prius and was settling himself into the front seat. "Was old Bob bothering you again? I've spoken to the principal about him. I don't like the way he talks to the girls. Always showing them his bulbs and clippings. Who knows what he'll be showing them next. Surely he's past his retirement age? The school needs a nice new gardener. There's a local firm I saw advertised in the paper. Girls in the Garden. Or was it Hotties in the Hawthorn? Either way, they'd fit in much better with our young ladies."

"Marcus. Can I help you?"

Marcus sneezed and sniffed back the drips. "You're driving up to school aren't you?"

"Yes."

"I thought I'd partake in a lift." He buckled himself in and sat taller in the seat. "I've been to see Angel again. She really does enjoy my company. It can't be fun working day in day out with just the local riff raff for company. I think I raise the clientele in that little establishment."

Susan touched the accelerator, silently starting the car. "Marcus, the Black Bear's older than the school. People travel for miles to experience its authenticity."

"Yes, but I bet they don't know it's actually an old coaching inn." He pulled on his ginger moustache. "In fact, it's the oldest working pub in the whole of Surrey."

"That's why they come!" Susan tutted. "What does it matter, anyway?"

"No need to get touchy just because I know more facts about our old English pub than you do. Not all of us are lucky enough to have a friend on the inside."

Susan pressed harder on the accelerator, unable to enjoy the rows of tall evergreen trees guiding them up the picturesque drive towards the square acre of grass that lay in front of the imposing school building. The students loved the open green space, and many could be found lazing there in the warm summer months, reading, chatting, or just absorbing the moment: their moment as a student at St Wilf's. Usually the sight of the acre, and the view of the impressive red-brick building behind it, made Susan smile in a quiet, contented, fashion, but today she simply wanted to park up and get Marcus out of the car.

"We're living the high life, Susan," said Marcus, flaring his nostrils with pride. "Working at St Wilfred's is an honour. An honour that has to be earned."

Susan turned left behind the main building and headed towards the staff car park, which was deliberately hidden from view. "People apply for the job as advertised in the TES, just like any other school."

"But they only take the best candidates here, Susan."

"And other schools don't?" Susan tightened her grip on the steering wheel. "Comprehensive schools employ the teacher who performs the most poorly on the day do they?"

Marcus shifted in his seat and angled his body towards Susan. "You really have got to control that little temper of yours, Susan. Us hot-blooded males like a bit of feistiness in our women, but you're bordering on snappy." He held the end of his nose as if he was about to sneeze again. "Yes, yes, yes … no, it's gone." He wiped a clear droplet from his nostril. "Oh I see! You thought I was referring to Jenna and the fact she thinks she can jump start her career here at St Wilfred's. Where is she by the way?"

Susan spotted a parking space and started to reverse. "You know where she is, Marcus. She's on her way back to Morzine. I've just dropped her off at the airport."

"Aha! That explains it then! No wonder you're all crotchety. What is it? The knowledge she'll have forgotten you by the time the plane lands, or the fact you *know* she's only been using you to get her School Direct training here at our prestigious establishment?"

"Marcus! She'll be a great teacher. You saw her in assembly. The girls were fixated by her every word."

"Only because the other lady was talking about her job in a sausage factory, and the man was talking about the excitement he has every day with data entry." Marcus unbuckled his seatbelt and placed a hand on Susan's knee. "Mon amie, I can forgive your little dalliance with lesbianism, and in fact I *have* questioned whether you initiated the whole thing to satisfy a desire you thought you saw in me. I'm your typical macho man. We have a reputation for liking a small portion of girl-on-girl action—"

"Marcus! Stop! Just stop!" Susan pulled her leg away from his podgy hand and pressed the park button, cutting all power to the car. "Jenna and I are in love. She's finishing the season, and then yes, we do hope she'll get her School Direct placement here, with a view to teaching here too."

"She's a brown-haired buxom beauty, Susan, and she's carefree on the slopes with the rest of her kind. You know the sort, all free love and whatnot. You're a thin-haired plain Jane who spends most of her time in the library. I mean, come on, you can't still believe she's attracted to you?"

Susan closed her eyes. "We're back, Marcus. Aren't you on duty this afternoon?"

"I love how you know my timetable, mon amie."

"It's Saturday. You're always on duty on Saturday."

Marcus grinned widely, displaying his small peg teeth in all their glory. "And I'm always done by seven p.m. if you fancy watching a film, or getting a bite to eat?"

"You've just called me a thin-haired plain Jane."

"Only in comparison to her mane of wild 'big hair', and charismatically dimpled cheeks, not to mention her huge bust and slim-line ski figure." Marcus paused for breath. "But you, Susan, you're much more my type."

"Marcus, I'm a lesbian."

"You've been a lesbian for two weeks. That hardly constitutes you joining the nunnery. Plus it's not like she'll be faithful. She'll be courting a different female's interest every evening. Ladies like her don't go three months without being attended to."

"Attended to? Marcus! Please!" Susan sighed. "You need to get to your duty."

"My mon amie, always thinking about others before thinking about herself." He ran his fingers through his thinning hair. "Put out of your mind the thought of the flirting. Put out of your mind the knowledge of the nookie. Put out of your mind the picture of her parallel turns as she skis the slopes with her secret smile."

"Could you get out of my car please?"

Marcus held onto the tip of his nose. "It's coming, it's coming, yes, yes, yes … no." He sniffed. "So are we on for tonight?"

Susan sighed. "You're not my type."

"Come on then, Rita Hayworth, what's wrong with me?"

"Marcus! Please! We've been through this a thousand times. We will never, *ever*, be a couple. Lesbianism aside."

Marcus lifted his nose. "A couple? I only asked you for a drink to offer my friendly shoulder whilst you wallowed in your misfortune of being used and abused by the gorgeous, and I mean far too gorgeous for you, Jenna James. Plus I've decided to pursue Angel from the Black Bear anyway, so this ship has sailed, sweetheart."

"Out," said Susan, pointing to the door.

"It's coming, it's coming, yes, yes, yes … achoo!" Marcus sneezed all over Susan's matte finish dashboard.

"For goodness sake, Marcus! Get a tissue from the glove box."

Marcus fumbled with the panel, tilting his head backwards to stop the remains of his sneeze dripping down his moustache. "Where's the handle?"

"Just tap it," said Susan, barely able to look at the scene.

Marcus banged on the glove box, sending Susan's two rubber dildos rolling onto his lap. "What in the name of great St Wilfred are these?" he gasped.

Susan watched open mouthed as he picked one up between his thumb and forefinger. "They're, they're—"

"They're a misrepresentation of the male form!" said Marcus, wiping his nose on his sleeve instead. "As if the penis is even half this size; and it's certainly not this wide!" He shook his head. "It's no wonder lesbians loathe men if this is what they're used to!"

Susan pointed at the glove box. "Just put them back, please."

Marcus dangled one above his head and slid his glasses further down his nose, peering at it closely. "I mean this girth's unfathomable."

"It's a standard six-inch vibrator, Marcus. Now put it back."

Marcus lifted the second one from his lap. "And this one's got buttons? Oh heavens above!" he squealed, as the blue one started to jolt up and down.

"Put them away!"

Marcus gently slapped it against his cheek. "Ooo, It generates quite a bit of power, doesn't it?"

Susan snatched the vibrators from his hands and pointed them towards the door. "Out! I mean it! Get out of my car."

"Be careful where you put those things, mon amie. You could cause someone an injury."

Susan banged them against the palm of her hand. "Out," she ordered.

CHAPTER FOUR

Susan waited for Marcus to disappear into the staff entrance at the back of the school before stepping out of her car. She was flustered and embarrassed, but more than anything, she was cross. How dare Marcus question Jenna's actions, and how dare he be so rude? Susan pressed the square key fob and heard her car lock behind her. She walked out of the car park the way she had driven in with the intention of entering the school through the grand entrance, hopefully avoiding any further contact with Marcus Ramsbottom. She crossed the gravel path and climbed the steps at the side of the building, giving her a perfect view out across the green acre. There were a few girls, wrapped up warm, kicking a ball around, and what looked like a couple of hockey players making their way back from the astro pitches on the other side of the road. Susan hugged her own shoulders. That was the one thing that Marcus *had* got right: his assessment of the weather. It was, in fact, colder than it had been up in the French Alps two weeks ago. Susan thought back to the way the sun had shone directly overhead, and the way Jenna had wrapped her arms around her from behind, planting small kisses up and down her neck. Susan paused her thought as she noticed little Daisy Button hobbling towards her on her crutches. Jenna had barely been gone an hour and already the daydreaming had begun. She smiled to herself. Who was she kidding? The daydreaming had begun the very first time she had laid eyes on her soon-to-be ski instructor at the French service station, and she had been re-living their first kiss, their first touch, ever since.

Susan quickened her pace along the elevated path that ran the length of the imposing building. "How did you manage those, Daisy?" she said, pointing towards the grand entrance and the twenty or so wide stone steps that led up to the huge oak doors.

"You always look happy now, Madam Quinn. You know that, right?" Daisy Button was looking up, trying to protect her pale eyes from the soft winter sun as she balanced one of her crutches under her arm.

Susan blushed. "Thank you, Daisy. You look happy too. But how did you get down those steps? And how's the leg in general?" Susan paused as the little girl with white hair and white skin continued to grin and nod in a knowing fashion. "How are things at home? And on that note, what's a day girl like you doing here on a Saturday? Have you joined a team? No, of course you haven't. You won't be out of plaster for another … four weeks, is it?"

"You're funny, Madam Quinn." Daisy was smiling from ear to ear. "You tell me why you're happy and I'll tell you why I'm happy."

Susan coughed and crouched down next to the little girl. "I'm happy that your leg's healing nicely."

Daisy continued to smile as she pushed her large, round prescription glasses further up her nose, staring at her teacher with eyes the size of saucers. "No you're not," she said, "you're happy because you're in love with Jenna."

"Daisy!" Susan rocked slightly as a gust of wind whipped across the quad and hit her at full force.

"You are! Everyone knows it and everyone's happy for you. I've started a petition that I'm going to take to Principal Cavanagh asking if Jenna can do her training here."

"Daisy, really there's no need. She's already submitted her School Direct application form."

"Every little helps though. The principal loves it when we give her feedback on things, and she needs to know how kind Jenna is and how good she was in our drama club last week, and she definitely needs to know how easy she is to talk to and how good she is at giving advice. Plus old Bob loves her and I love Timmy, so if I get Jenna a job here then Bob will love me, and he'll tell Timmy how nice I am too."

Susan frowned. "Timmy? Bob the groundsman's grandson?"

"He's eleven like me. He helps with the planting at the weekends." Daisy smiled even wider. "I think he likes me."

"So *that's* why you're here on a Saturday."

Daisy nodded enthusiastically. "I want to ask him out, but I'm scared he'll say no. Some of the other girls like him and they said there's no way he'd ever go out with an albino girl." She shrugged her shoulders. "They said it would be like Justin Bieber going out with a bag of flour."

Susan shook her head. "A bag of flour? How ridiculous."

"Or Casper the Ghost. Sometimes they just call me Blizzard."

"Oh Daisy, you all got on so well in Morzine. Would you like me to report it, or try and sort it out?"

"No, it's some of the other girls. The smokers."

"Smokers!? You know that's cause for instant suspension here at St Wilfred's. Who are these girls? Where do they smoke? Tell me their—"

"No, Madam Quinn, it's fine. I talked to Jenna about it yesterday. She's given me a plan and I'm sure it'll work."

Susan stood back up and folded her arms. "No, I'm not happy about this. It's cold. Shall we go inside and have a chat?"

"No, I spoke to Jenna. I'm fine."

"Those girls will be in a lot of trouble if they get caught smoking, and it may make them think twice about their other silly behaviour."

"Please, Madam Quinn. It's fine. I'm happy." Daisy smiled. "Just like you're happy." She nodded towards the huge winding driveway. "And anyway, I'm off to help Timmy. He's joining Bob in a bit and we're planting some bulbs. He said my crutch would be good for poking holes in the soil."

Susan smiled. "That sounds great. But only if you're sure, Daisy?"

"I'm fine."

"Okay. Have fun, and don't let yourself get too cold."

Daisy grinned. "I won't. Last time Timmy lent me his jacket."

"Oh Daisy, that does sound promising."

"I know, and with Jenna's plan I'm sure he'll be asking me out in no time!"

Susan nodded. "Right, well next time I talk to Jenna I'll make sure she fills me in on this plan of hers."

"Bye, Madam Quinn," said Daisy, repositioning her crutches and starting her long walk down the wide path.

Susan shouted after her. "Do you want me to get my car and drive you down there?"

"No," said Daisy over her shoulder. "The cold air might put a bit of colour in my cheeks."

"Oh bless," said Susan under her breath, smiling at the white glow that seemed to surround the little girl wherever she went.

Daisy shouted one final time. "Your smile suits you."

"Yours too," said Susan, turning around and walking as quickly as she could along the path. She had never been one of these teachers who ran frantically around the school site, no matter how late or cold she was. It had always been important to Susan to behave in a highly appropriate and somewhat standoffish manner in school, and this used to include her limited interactions with the girls. She had always felt respected, but never particularly well liked. The ski trip and influence of Jenna James had changed that completely and she had started to realise that the girls at St Wilfred's liked, and actually needed, a more personal approach.

Susan nodded to herself. A week of teaching had passed since the trip and nothing dreadful had happened. The girls weren't rioting in her classes now they knew a little bit more about her private life. The teachers weren't shunning her in the staffroom. There hadn't been a drop in lesson productivity or pupil performance. She smiled to herself. There had just been a notable rise in the amount of personal interactions she had experienced and words of kindness she had received. Susan took a deep breath and gave herself one final nod as she passed under the huge stone pillars and pushed her way through the sturdy oak doors into the grand entrance of St Wilfred's All-Girls School.

"Ah, Susan, could we have a word, please?" The school's new, yet well respected, principal, Ellen Cavanagh, was emerging from her office with her second in command, the very old and very uptight vice principal, Dorothy Brown.

"It's more than a word, isn't it, Principal Cavanagh?" Dorothy Brown was frowning at the much younger woman who'd cheated her out of the job she'd spent forty years working towards. "I like to think of it as the implementation of an investigation."

Ellen Cavanagh smiled politely. "Dorothy, we're merely fact finding, and please, I keep telling you to call me Ellen."

"I'll do no such thing. Principal Jackson spent the last twenty years maintaining the school's historic and celebrated tradition of appropriate etiquette and I'll continue to do my part for my final few months," she nodded, wobbling her jowls, "just as I've done for my forty years here at St Wilfred's."

Susan stood still and smiled with slight worry. "How can I help?"

"Let's go to my office," said Ellen.

"No, I think we should go to mine," said Dorothy, turning on her heels and marching down the wide oak corridor, past painting after painting of every school principal since Elizabeth Warwick, 1854–1861.

Ellen Cavanagh and Susan Quinn followed the formidable woman as quickly as they could, both noticing the way her head was held high, as if saluting each of the portraits she passed.

"Needs a polish," said Dorothy Brown, tutting as she pointed her finger towards the large trophy cabinet, but not slowing her pace. She lifted her head back up and marched past the paintings of Edward Sears, 1922–1929, and Celia Monkton, 1929–1931, stopping momentarily to snap at a student on the other side of the corridor who was standing too close to the school's impressive display of white marble busts. "Don't touch!" she shouted.

Susan kept up her pace, but noticed that Dorothy slowed as she approached the large painting of the school's late principal, Richard Jackson, 1993–2013.

She spotted the curtsey.

Ellen turned to Susan and smiled. "I'm sitting for my portrait next week."

Dorothy Brown stopped abruptly and span back around. "I do hope you're using the school's resident painter and not some new-fangled art deco type?"

"Yes, and I'm keeping with tradition. I'll be painted in the Great Hall, just like all of the other principals."

Dorothy nodded and continued her walk, sniffing as she spoke. "I always pictured myself up here."

"You would have made a fantastic principal, Dorothy."

Dorothy Brown stopped her walk once again and stared at the younger woman. "If that were the case they wouldn't have given the job to you. I maintain that sixty five is *not* too old to take the helm here at St Wilfred's."

Ellen placed a friendly hand on Dorothy's shoulder. "I'm honoured to have you as my second in command."

"Well, make the most of it. It's only a matter of months until my forced retirement." Dorothy shook her head. "But don't you worry. I'll be making damn sure I clean up as much as I can before they clear me out. This investigation will give a much needed warning signal to any members of staff who think they can get away with blue murder just because you're new." Dorothy Brown shook her head even harder. "And god-forbid what will happen if my replacement's as young as you are."

"Dorothy. I'm thirty nine. This is my second post as principal and my second term here."

"Well I've been teaching at St Wilfred's for forty years and in my day you chose a school and you stuck with it. There wasn't any of this skipping around from post to post, using each educational establishment to better yourself. In my day we tried to better the educational establishment we worked in. The educational establishment we committed to. The educational establishment we dedicated our lives to."

"Dorothy, your passion is remarkable and, like you, I plan on staying here at St Wilfred's for a very long time."

"Providing the place doesn't crumble around you."

"Excuse me?" said Ellen.

Dorothy threw her hands to her hips. "Principal Cavanagh, let me take the lead on this investigation. I'll show you how it's done. I've been watching you. You need to instil more fear in your staff. You need to show them who's boss. You need to make them realise that behaviour like this, will simply *not* be tolerated."

Susan spoke quietly. "Should I be worried?"

CHAPTER FIVE

Susan looked around the old-fashioned office, quite unsure what to focus on. Dorothy Brown had taken the helm in her walnut and hide desk chair, which was clearly an antique in its own right, whilst Ellen Cavanagh had chosen to sit down on the wooden pew at the side of the room, as if distancing herself from the upcoming course of events. Susan glanced at the two uncomfortable looking chairs in front of Dorothy's desk and wondered whether to take a seat, but thought better of it and looked out of the large sash window instead. The view over the acre was incredible. Susan spotted the same group of girls still kicking the ball around, and from her elevated position she could see over the trees and across the driveway to the four large astro pitches where two rival schools were pitting their skills against St Wilfred's in games of hockey and lacrosse.

"You may take a seat, Madam Quinn." Dorothy Brown angled her nod towards Ellen, as if confirming the authority she still commanded with the staff.

Susan stepped forwards and sat quickly, crossing her legs at the ankles and tucking them under her chair, suddenly more conscious of her causal weekend attire. "How can I help you, Vice Principal Brown?"

Dorothy Brown glanced at Ellen again and nodded at the respect she'd been given. "I'm opening an investigation."

Susan knew better than to comment, so she sat still and held her breath, desperately trying to ignore all of the thoughts racing through her head. Was this about Jenna? About their relationship? Had a parent complained? Had she crossed the line with her openness? Had Jenna crossed the line? Had Jenna been too modern in her approach to the lessons she'd helped out with? Was their relationship frowned upon? Was she about to get fired?

"It's Professor Ramsbottom."

"Marcus?" said Susan confused.

Dorothy Brown nodded. "We're investigating."

"We're fact finding," said Ellen from the other side of the room.

"Principal Cavanagh. Please allow me to have my final triumph, my final moment at the helm, my final—"

"Dorothy, you're not retiring until the summer."

"Two terms." Dorothy shook her head. "I have two terms in which to leave my legacy. Two terms to get this place back on the straight and narrow. Two terms to show you how things are done." She coughed lightly, regaining control of herself for a moment. "I don't mean any offence, Principal Cavanagh, but there's so much tradition here that's simply at risk."

Ellen Cavanagh stood from her seat and took the chair next to Susan. She lifted it up and walked to the side of Dorothy's desk. "Dorothy, I've said this before and I'll say it again," she glanced at Susan and smiled, "and I don't mind other members of staff hearing this, because it can't be said enough." Ellen took a deep breath, betraying the fact that she felt like she'd already said it enough. "I am *wholeheartedly* committed to the values instilled and upheld by you and the wonderful teachers here at St Wilfred's. From what I have heard, Principal Jackson was a magnificent man, and the two of you guided this school through many a successful year." She smiled at Dorothy and sat down. "I value and respect the heritage here at St Wilfred's and I intend on maintaining the long line of custom and tradition that this school holds dear—"

"So let me get rid of that dreadful little man!"

"Dorothy!"

"I'm sorry, Principal Cavanagh, but he simply isn't a good enough fit."

Ellen turned to Susan. "I do apologise. We've had a parental complaint about Marcus Ramsbottom and we need to iron out a couple of issues."

"No, we need to turn up the steam setting and slam that iron down, firing out the creases as we go." Dorothy was banging her fist on the desk. "I've never liked him with his smart remarks and air of—"

"He's been here for seven years, Dorothy." Ellen paused and turned to Susan. "I'm sorry. Could you give us a minute, please?"

Susan nodded and stood from her chair, walking out of the office and closing the heavy door behind her. She waited in the corridor, listening as best she could, even though she had a fair idea of how the conversation inside might go. Ellen Cavanagh had been a wonderful addition to the school following the sudden death of Principal Jackson last year. Yes, she'd had a hard act to follow, but for the most part she was excelling. The staff and students were showing her respect, and she'd already got the parents on board with her mix of new initiatives that supplemented the old school traditions. Yes, thought Susan, Ellen was getting it right, even when it came to old Dorothy Brown. Everybody knew that Dorothy had applied for the job as principal, only to be offered her retirement instead. She was a patron of St Wilfred's and was finding it hard to grasp the idea of life without the institution, hence her new boss's delicate handling of her somewhat erratic behaviour.

Susan stepped away from the door as it opened with a creak. "Shall I come back in?"

Ellen smiled. "Yes, sorry." She lowered her voice. "Dorothy *will* be taking charge on this one, but please don't feel pressured into her way of thinking. We need facts, not opinions."

"PLEASE ENTER," shouted Dorothy.

Susan stepped back into the office, noticing the old woman's red cheeks and sweaty brow, possibly the result of the firm but fair dressing down by her younger, much calmer, boss. "How can I help, Vice Principal Brown?"

Dorothy lifted her piece of paper off the desk and squinted at the hand written letter. "Can you please tell me how on earth Eugenie Rohampton managed to see, and I quote, Professor Ramsbottom's ginger bum pubes?"

"Pardon?"

"On your ski trip. I have a letter here from Mr Rohampton, who might I add is a huge benefactor here at St Wilfred's. He says," she paused to pull the piece of paper even closer, "my daughter thoroughly enjoyed the school ski trip organised by the very wonderful Madam Quinn, but I'm concerned that her highlight seems to be the public viewing of Professor Ramsbottom's ginger bum pubes."

Susan spoke quietly. "Is there humour in his tone?"

"Would you be laughing if your daughter attended one of the country's top fee-paying all-girls schools and was exposed to such horrors?"

Susan swallowed. "Does he go on to make a complaint?"

"The official parental complaint isn't from Mr Rohampton, but he's drawn yet another misdemeanour to our attention. It needs to be investigated, as do a number of other issues that I'm not willing to disclose at this time. I've been keeping a record on that man ever since he tried, unsuccessfully might I add, to show me up in assembly back in 2008." Dorothy Brown shook her head at the memory. "What I need from you, Madam Quinn, is a clear and concise written account of Professor Ramsbottom's behaviour on your trip."

Ellen Cavanagh turned to Susan and smiled. "But as Mr Rohampton said, the trip was a huge success and we're very grateful for all of your hard work."

Dorothy Brown mumbled. "Yes, that too."

CHAPTER SIX

Susan was lying on her bed staring at the ceiling. It was 9.00 p.m. and she could hear the resident housemistress blowing her whistle, no doubt trying to regain order on a typical Saturday night where the girls would push boundaries and try to stay up later than allowed. Susan's single-room apartment was in the centre of the staff living quarters, and was far enough away from the dorms for her to feel her freedom, but close enough for her to offer assistance when needed. It wasn't in her remit to help out in the evenings, the school employed four live-in housemistresses and a head of boarding for that, but sometimes she did find herself coming to the rescue when drama or emotion took over. Not tonight though, she thought, checking her clock once more. She sighed, finding it hard to believe that Jenna had woken up beside her, but was now more than a thousand miles away. Her stomach lunged as she relived their morning of passion. Both had known it would be a while before they'd enjoy each other again, and this had added an intensely emotional element to their love making, seemingly impossible given that every encounter of theirs was already highly charged. Susan closed her eyes and remembered, suddenly jumping at the sound of her phone. She blinked quickly and looked at the screen. Jenna's photo was smiling out at her and the text was telling her that: Jenna James would like to FaceTime. Susan looked at the two buttons at the bottom: one red with a line through the video camera and the word *decline*, one green with a video camera, no line, and the word *accept*. She clicked on the green *accept* button and brought the phone up to her ear.

"Hello."

"Susan? Hi! Can you see me?"

Susan instinctively glanced around the room. "No."

"It's FaceTime, Susan. You should be able to see me. You've not got the phone to your ear have you?"

Susan sheepishly adjusted her position, spotting Jenna smiling and waving. "Jenna! Wow! Hi! How are you? This is weird. I feel embarrassed."

"Stop it, Susan! You must have done FaceTime before?"

Susan shook her head, trying not to focus on the small moving image of herself in the bottom right hand corner of the phone. "Am I big on your screen?"

"Yes," said Jenna, "and I can see you checking yourself out. Try and look into the camera if you can."

Susan lifted her eyes and looked at Jenna who was staring straight at her, smiling and displaying her gorgeous dimple and big brown eyes in all their glory. "You look beautiful, Jenna."

"That's kind because I feel totally shattered."

"How was your flight?" asked Susan, unable to resist the temptation of a quick glance down at herself again.

Jenna waited for Susan to finish straightening her hair. "You look gorgeous, Susan, and just so you know, I'm hoping to see you far more dishevelled than this at some point on FaceTime in the not too distant future."

"Is it safe?" asked Susan.

"What?"

"FaceTime. Is it safe? Could people be watching us right now?"

Jenna laughed. "No, of course not. Who would want to anyway?"

"What if the girls in the dorms had their Wi-Fi or Bluetooth on? Could they log in and watch this?"

Jenna pulled down her grey v-neck jumper and popped a boob out of her bra. "No," she said, "we're perfectly safe."

"Jenna!"

"What?"

Susan lowered her voice. "You can't sit there and talk to me with your boob hanging out!"

Jenna nodded. "Actually, you're right. Give me a second."

Susan watched as the image on the screen did a 90 degree flip, giving her a momentary view of Jenna's ceiling. "Can you still hear me?" she shouted, "how was the flight?"

Jenna appeared back on the screen. "There's no need to shout, Susan, I'm still here."

Susan gasped at the image of Jenna, completely naked on her top half. "Jenna!"

"What? I miss you."

"I miss you too," said Susan, her eyes drawn to Jenna's firm stomach and pert breasts. "Is it cold?" she asked with the trace of a smile.

Jenna slowly ran a finger across her collarbone and down her chest, lightly flicking her hard nipple as she continued the route down to her stomach. "No, I'm just turned on."

"Jenna!"

"What, Susan? I spent the whole journey replaying what we got up to this morning."

Susan felt her stomach lunge again. "Actually, I was thinking the same thing when you called."

"And?"

"And what?"

Jenna stared directly into the camera. "Did it turn you on?"

Susan felt the butterflies of anticipation flutter across her chest. "Yes. Thinking about you always turns me on."

"What in particular?"

Susan glanced around her room. "Can you walk and talk for a minute? I need to close the curtains."

"Ooo, I like the sound of this," said Jenna, re-adjusting her own position.

Susan held the phone at arm's length as she hopped off her bed and walked towards her open-plan kitchen. Her apartment was small and basic, but had everything she needed, and over time she'd managed to make the space feel very personal, and incredibly homely. The room wasn't quite themed but there was a definite influence from the two summers she'd spent in Morocco. The walls were a warm cinnamon red, accessorised with a couple of brightly coloured throws and intricately patterned canvases. Her favourite thing though was the dark brown Moroccan pendant lamp she'd shipped over, which added its own intricate design of light and shade to the richly coloured walls.

Susan had a double bed covered by another bright throw, and an old-fashioned wardrobe and chest of drawers, slightly hidden by the apartment's L-shaped layout. There was a basic kitchen in the centre of the main area with two stools and a tall countertop, where she did most of her eating, and marking. The living space was next to the window and it consisted of a sofa, coffee table and small TV.

Susan glanced at her phone as she passed the counter and knelt on the sofa, pulling the curtains closed with one hand. "What are you doing?" she asked, seeing Jenna moving around on the screen.

"Getting myself comfortable."

"For what?"

Jenna was smiling. "You know what, now go and make sure your door's locked."

Susan turned back around and headed for the door, already sure that the latch was on. She dimmed the lights and made her way back to her bed. "Do I have to hold this phone up the whole time?"

"No," said Jenna, "you'll need both of your hands."

Susan felt a surge of anticipation. "Where shall I put it?"

"Stand it up on the chest of drawers next to your bed."

"My cabinet?"

"No, the chest of drawers I fucked you against this morning."

"Jenna!"

"What? I did. Rest the phone on there. I want to talk to you properly."

Susan smiled. "Good, I'm glad we're talking. Tell me about your journey."

Jenna propped herself onto an elbow. "It was fine. Good flight. Good transfer. But I missed you."

Susan made one final adjustment to her phone's position and climbed onto the bed, checking the small box in the corner to make sure Jenna would be able to see exactly what she wanted to see. "Is this okay?"

"It's perfect," said Jenna. "Now take off your top."

Susan swallowed. "You're sure it's safe?"

"Positive. I want to see you."

Susan slowly undid the top button of her shirt. "How much do you want to see?"

"Do you have any idea how sexy you are, Madam Quinn?"

Susan undid another button, pulling the shirt wider. "You make me feel sexy."

"You are. Look at you. Take it off completely."

Susan did as instructed, propping herself up against her pillow and displaying her lacy black bra. "I wish you were here, Jenna."

"So do I, but I'm not, so I'll have to give you the next best thing."

"And what's that?" asked Susan.

"I want you to come for me."

"On my own?"

"No, I'm going to talk to you. I'm going to tell you what I'd do to you if I was there, and I just want you to close your eyes and enjoy the moment."

"You're *sure* it's safe?"

"I promise you it's safe. Just close your eyes and relax. Imagine it's me lying on the bed next to you. Imagine my breasts pressing into the side of your body. Feel my nipples hard against yours."

Susan closed her eyes and moaned, remembering the way their bodies seemed to fit together perfectly. "I love your nipples, Jenna."

"Good, because I'm touching them, right now, for you."

Susan opened her eyes and looked at the screen. Jenna was lying on her back with her nipples between her fingers. Susan gasped. "Squeeze them for me."

Jenna looked at the screen and smiled. "You're meant to be relaxing."

"But you're so hot. You're turning me on. How am I meant to relax knowing you're lying there doing that?"

Jenna pulled on her nipples and started to moan. "If you were here I'd ask for it hard and fast."

Susan moved closer to the screen. "Touch yourself for me."

"I will, but I'm going to touch myself as I talk to you. We'll come together." She smiled at Susan. "Lie down. I'm going to describe exactly what I want to do to your body."

Susan groaned. She loved everything Jenna did to her body. Jenna was so confident in bed, and so adventurous in her demands that nothing was ever repetitive or habitual. Every single encounter had been wonderfully unique. Susan closed her eyes, excitedly anticipating this latest innovative experience. "Okay, what do you want me to do?"

"Hang on, before we start, how was the rest of your day?" Jenna was smiling. "Sorry I haven't asked you yet. That was really rude of me."

Susan lifted herself back off the bed. "It wasn't as exciting as this is going to be. Come on, I'm ready. What do you want me to do?"

"Okay, lie back down."

Susan popped her head back up. "Ooo, but remind me to talk about Daisy Button and Marcus."

"What about Daisy Button and Marcus?"

"I'll tell you afterwards. Come on. I'm ready."

Jenna laughed. "Okay. Here goes. Close your eyes."

"They're closed."

"And just listen."

"I'm listening." Susan smiled.

"Susan, you have to take this seriously."

"I am!" said Susan. "Come on, I want to see if you're as good as you think you are."

"What do you mean by that?"

Susan sat back up. "You're a thousand miles away. It's hardly going to feel the same is it."

"Right, lady, lie down."

Susan giggled. "I love it when you're firm."

"Do you now?" asked Jenna.

"Mmm hmm."

"Okay then. Imagine this." Jenna lowered her voice. "We're living together—"

"Since when?"

"Just go with it!"

Susan snuggled down into the bed. "Okay, we're living together."

"You've spent the day teasing me on the text and being cheeky, just like you're being cheeky now."

"Okay."

"Shh!" said Jenna

"Sorry."

"So, I send you a message. Telling you to be prepared for when I get home." Jenna paused, waiting for the smart remark, but when it didn't come she carried on. "So, I tell you I'm going to take you, the minute I walk through the door."

Susan moaned. "Mmm."

"You like that don't you. The idea of me taking control."

Susan moaned again.

"I tell you I want you waiting naked on the bed. Exactly like you are now."

"I've still got my trousers on."

"Well take them off," said Jenna. "I need you naked."

Susan hastily unbuttoned her jeans and kicked them off at the ankle.

"Bra, pants, and socks too. Don't forget I can see you, Susan."

Susan pulled off her underwear and threw it to the floor. She glanced at her phone, suddenly feeling incredibly vulnerable. "Can you see everything?" she asked.

"Yes," said Jenna, "and that's exactly how I'd need you to be. Naked and waiting."

"So," said Susan, "I'm naked and waiting. Now what?"

"Close your eyes."

"Why?"

"Because I've just walked into the room and I've taken off my silk scarf. I've tied it tightly around your eyes."

"Ooo, the nice one with the butterflies?"

"Susan! Please!"

"Sorry."

"So, you're on the bed, naked, blindfolded, and I tell you not to talk. I tell you to listen." Jenna paused, pleased with the silence. "Imagine I'm wearing that pale blue denim shirt you love."

"With those black Gap jeans?"

"Yes, whatever, it doesn't matter. Anyway, you're listening and you hear me slowly unbuttoning my shirt, one button at a time."

Susan giggled.

"What?!"

"Is there any other way to unbutton a shirt?"

"I don't know, but I'm doing it slowly and sexily." She paused. Susan was quiet. "You can hear the zip on my jeans slowly opening all of the way. The clip of my bra as my breasts fall free. The sound of my knickers rolling down my thighs."

"That would be silent."

"Susan!"

"What?"

"Right, that's it," said Jenna. "You know what I'd really do if I was there right now? I'd take that scarf off your eyes and pull your arms behind your back. I'd tie you at the wrist and I'd drag your body to the end of the bed, dropping you onto your knees on the floor. I'd push on your back so you were face first in the mattress, your arse pointing at me."

"Ooo, I like this."

"Yeah? Well guess what? You'd think you were about to get fucked. You'd think I was about to come behind you and plunge my fingers deep inside you. You'd think I was about to press my nipples into your back, forcing you down on the bed as I rammed harder into you, fucking your clit and bringing you close to orgasm."

"Mmm, Jenna."

"But I wouldn't. I'd step over your head instead, sitting myself down on the bed right in front of your face. Your hands would be tied so you wouldn't be able to touch me. You'd just see me. I'd be naked. You'd see my wetness. You'd look up and see me playing with my nipples. You'd try and stand, but I'd wrap my legs around your back, pinning you down into position with my heels."

"This is hot."

"Touch yourself as I talk, Susan. Imagine this is really happening."

Susan moved one hand to her breast and one between her legs, aware that her body already thought it *was* happening. "Keep going," she said, starting to make small circles with her fingers.

"You're watching me as I arouse myself. I'm pulling on my nipples and making them really hard. I'm squeezing them and moaning out in desire. You see me, inches away, wet and waiting. You try and move forwards with your mouth. You're desperate to taste me. Desperate to feel my wetness on your tongue, but I move backwards. This is about me now. Not you. I trail my fingers down my stomach, really slowly. You watch as I close my eyes, getting carried away. You see me parting my legs wider. I'm completely open. I'm right in front of you. You moan as you imagine your fingers in me. Your tongue parting me. But instead you watch as I slam my own fingers deep inside. I push them hard. Really hard." Jenna swallowed as she watched the image on her screen. Susan was doing exactly the same thing to herself, pushing her fingers as deep as they'd go. Jenna gasped and continued to talk. "You see me fucking my fingers so hard into myself, but I tell you I want more. I tell you I need more. You look up at me, helpless, expecting me to untie you, but I don't. Instead I take the back of your head and force you forward onto me. I tilt my pelvis up to you and use your tongue for my own pleasure. My heels are in your back and my pussy's in your face and—"

"Jenna!!" gasped Susan. "I just came!"

Jenna swallowed, quickening the pace with her own fingers. "Tell me how it felt. I'm really close as well."

Susan rolled onto her side and watched Jenna writhing around on the small screen. "Come for me, Jenna. I want you to come for me, because what happens next, is me, ripping the silk scarf free from my wrists. I rip it free and I pin you down by your shoulders. I straddle your chest, bringing my wetness up to your mouth. I lean backwards and reach down with my fingers. I push them inside you. I bring you so close before—"

"Fuckkkk!"

"Wait! I haven't finished my scenario yet!"

"Fuck!" said Jenna, shuddering with the contractions. "You just made me come!"

"I didn't get chance to do anything!"

Jenna moaned with satisfaction. "You did. I was watching you. I was watching you touch yourself. I was watching you bite your bottom lip. I was watching you push your fingers deep inside."

Susan giggled. "Crikey that was good."

"I think we did okay for our first attempt," laughed Jenna.

"Sorry, I get it now. No questioning, just go with the flow."

Jenna smiled at Susan's red cheeks. "You're so gorgeous, Susan, and I'm completely and utterly head over heels in love with you."

"I miss you."

"I miss you too," said Jenna, "but when you know you know, and you know we're going to make it."

"I know we will," said Susan with a smile. She paused. "Is that someone knocking?"

Jenna tilted her head. "They'll go away."

"It might be Sylvie. Say hello to her for me, would you?"

Jenna sat up as the knocking got louder. "I'm not at Sylvie's this week. I'm at the chalet."

"The ski rep chalet?"

"Yep. I'm playing guide to a group of execs this week."

"Oh right." Susan heard the knocking again. "Hadn't you better answer the door though?"

"No, it's fine. I'm still basking in the afterglow of that incredible orgasm you just gave me."

"It might be important. Are you expecting anyone?"

Jenna shook her head. "No."

"Go and answer the door. I'll wait."

"Ugh, it won't be important," said Jenna, reaching down for her jumper and climbing off the bed.

Susan watched Jenna disappear out of view and wondered how she hadn't noticed the absence of Sylvie's old-fashioned wallpaper. "Aren't you going to put on your pants?" she shouted.

"Maybe," said Jenna, momentarily popping her head back into the screen. "Give me a second."

Susan dropped her feet off the bed and drew herself closer to the phone, closing her eyes and trying to listen as best she could. Jenna was talking and laughing and someone was shouting in a high-pitched excitable voice. Susan brought her ear as close to the screen as she could, making out the words, "*Party, party, party,*" and, "*She's back! The lady's back in town!*"

"Why's your earlobe filling my phone, Susan?"

Susan jumped backwards and looked at Jenna smiling on the screen. "Who was that?"

"Amber."

"Amber?"

"Yes, we're all heading out in a bit."

"Now?"

"Yes, what are you up to tonight?"

Susan glanced at the clock. "It's nine thirty."

"Ten thirty here."

"But Amber? I thought—"

"Hey, life's too short to hold grudges. She apologised on the way up."

"You've been with Amber?"

"I caught a lift from the airport with her school. Poor thing's got another rough comp this week. We picked her up at the services."

Susan grabbed her shirt from the floor and held it against her bare chest. "Jenna! Don't you remember how mean she was to me? Don't you remember what she said?"

"She was drunk, Susan. She's apologised."

"Not to me she hasn't."

"Shall I call her back in? She really was embarrassed about her behaviour. She literally begged for forgiveness. Hey, and listen, she's not the first person to get rip roaring drunk and say something bad."

"But she was horrible. She was totally mean."

"I know, but she's sorry. Life's too short. Let me call her in."

"No!" gasped Susan, quite unsure what to make of the whole situation. "Let me get this right. It's your first night back, and you're going out with Amber?"

"Yes, and some others. Why? What are you up to?"

Susan looked at the clock again. "It's nine thirty!"

"Exactly. The night's young. There's no school tomorrow. What are your plans?"

Susan swallowed. "Is it wrong that I'm feeling a bit uncomfortable with this?"

"With what? With me going out?"

"No, with you going out with Amber."

Jenna sighed. "Do we need to talk about this?"

"Was that a sigh?"

"What?"

Susan nodded. "You sighed."

"What do you want me to say? She's a friend. She's a colleague. She'll be out and about lots over the next few months."

Susan closed her eyes and shook her head. "Look at me. I'm annoying you already."

"You're not annoying me, Susan, but you said you trusted me. I've told you that Amber won't be a problem."

"I do trust you. I don't trust her."

"It's fine. I'll text you when I get in." Jenna smiled. "Come on, tell me what you're up to tonight. Your turn to make me jealous."

Susan paused. "I don't know. Umm, I might see who's about in the communal lounge, or—"

"What do you usually do on a Saturday night?"

"Umm, well I tend to catch up on any marking I'm behind with, or—"

"Oh get yourself down to the Black Bear, Susan. I don't want you sitting around obsessing about what I'm getting up to, or what time I'll be back in."

"You think I obsess?"

"No, I didn't mean it like that. I just want you to have fun."

Susan shrugged her shoulders. "With who?"

"Who do you usually have fun with?"

Susan took her eyes away from the screen. "It's fine. I'll see if anyone wants to go for a drink."

"Aren't you on Facebook? Amber was telling me there's a new feature that shows which of your friends are close by. See who's around. Go have some fun."

"Jenna, I set up my profile years ago and I only had two friends then. I wouldn't have a clue what my password was or how to get back on there. And anyway, why would I want to join? You're not on there."

"I know! Far too many skeletons in far too many closets for that."

Susan frowned. "Was Amber trying to persuade you to join so she could keep track of your movements and bump into you all of the time?"

"No! She just mentioned it, so I thought I'd mention it to you."

"I'm fine. I've got friends."

"Good, so call them up and keep yourself busy for the next three months."

"I will. Don't worry about me."

Jenna nodded. "Good, and you don't worry about me either."

Susan frowned. "Is this what this is? You're worried I'm going to be sitting at home all alone, obsessing about the fun you're having, so you want me to go out and have some fun of my own?"

Jenna sighed. "No. I just asked what you were up to tonight."

"You're sighing again. Oh my goodness, I'm annoying you. Right, don't worry, I'm reactivating my Facebook account and I'll have a different activity lined up for every single evening." Susan smiled. "I'm not even sure I'll have time for any more sex-scenario sessions with you, sorry."

"Oh I love you, Susan Quinn."

Susan sniffed. "Just don't feel sorry for me."

"I don't."

"How about we both join Facebook as another way of keeping in contact?"

Jenna clenched her jaw. "No way. That site has two purposes. One is for boasting, like … *Ooo look at my new car and my big house and haven't I aged well, selfie, selfie, selfie …* and the other is for moaning, like … *What are you talking behind my back for? Karma's gunna get you, bitch!*"

Susan laughed. "It's not all like that."

"It is, and I've got enough friends already."

"And I haven't?"

"No, I didn't mean it like that." Jenna sighed. "Listen I have to go, but I'll give you a call tomorrow."

"Stop sighing! I'm sorry. I just hate the fact you're not here."

"We'll get through this," said Jenna. "We'll be fine."

"Yeah?"

"We will!"

Susan rubbed the sides of her face. "I know, I know, I know, I'm sorry. Right, you have a great evening and I'll speak to you tomorrow." She paused. "Text me when you get in though, just so I know that you're safe."

"Yes, boss," said Jenna, saluting her own forehead.

"Okay, have fun. I love you."

Jenna moved her lips into the screen. "I love you too."

Susan lifted the phone and brought it to her own mouth. She kissed the lips. "I love you more," she said before realising she'd somehow managed to hang up.

CHAPTER SEVEN

Susan pulled her clothes on and checked the star-shaped clock hanging on the wall next to her shelf of perfectly polished thimbles: Jenna's recent gift now taking centre stage. It was 9.45 p.m., and usually she'd be winding down, or maybe even turning in, but she didn't want Jenna to think she had absolutely no life whatsoever, so she slipped on her shoes and unlocked her apartment door, heading down the corridor towards the staff lounge. There were six other ground floor apartments in her living quarters and all had access to the shared communal area, which was incredibly old-fashioned and always smelt like a charity shop. She pushed open the door and was hit by the immediate fustiness. Susan walked inside and let her eyes adjust to the poorly lit room. Mel Copeland, the school's live-in PE teacher, was feet up, head back, snoring loudly on one of the sunken couches. Mary Llewellyn and Martha Adams, two of the school's oldest members of staff, were bent over a game of chess, and Danielle Watts, the school nurse, was tucking into what looked like her third bag of family-sized chocolate treats, and laughing loudly at a rerun of *Dad's Army*.

Susan edged past a couple of clothes horses that were weighed down with damp hockey shirts and socks. She stumbled slightly as she failed to spot the large bag of lacrosse sticks left open on the floor. Susan took a seat next to Danielle and glanced at the television. "I used to watch this when I was younger," she said, with a smile.

Danielle offered out a bag of toffees. "Never gets old."

Susan took one and started to chew, wondering how best to sound casual, yet appealing. "Finishes at ten, doesn't it?"

"Yeah," said Danielle, reaching down for her large glass of cola.

Susan paused. "The Black Bear usually has a musician playing on a Saturday night."

"Does it?"

Susan stretched out her arms and sucked on her lips. "I feel in the mood for something, but I'm not quite sure what."

Danielle offered the bag of Cadbury Clusters. Susan shook her head so Danielle reached down and lifted the half empty family bag of spicy tortilla chips, offering them out instead.

"No," said Susan, "I think I might fancy a drink."

Danielle passed over her glass of cola. "Or I've got some Fanta in the fridge if you prefer that? Might be a bit flat though."

Susan tapped her teeth together. "No, I think I'm fancying something a little bit stronger."

Old Martha Adams lifted her head from the chess board and reached into the pocket of her long cardigan. "Heads up," she shouted, as she threw over the small silver hip flask.

Susan missed the catch and flinched as the flask hit her on the knee. "Thanks," she said, not daring to open the lid and find out what was inside. She took a deep breath. "We could head up for last orders if any one fancies it?"

No one spoke.

"The musician will be on for another hour at least."

Danielle popped a couple of chocolate eclairs into her mouth. "No, it's only on for half an hour. Mmm." She chewed noisily. "It starts at ten."

"What does?" Susan frowned.

"The results show. Mmm. The Voice. That lady with the specs is just awful! Mmm. She's got to go!"

Susan shook her head. "No, I mean the musician at the Black Bear."

Danielle swallowed. "What musician?"

"The one at the Black Bear. Shall we go and maybe catch the last hour? We could walk down? I'll buy the drinks."

Danielle snorted. "Ha. Now?"

"I'm serious. I've heard the music's really good."

Danielle delved into her bag of pick and mix. "Too cold. Too late. Too weird at ten p.m. on a Saturday night."

Susan nodded. "Just a thought." She twisted back around on the couch and stretched out her legs, finally looking up at the two elderly women. "I don't suppose you two fancy a drink after that game of chess do you? I could order us a taxi so you wouldn't have to walk up the drive."

Mary Llewellyn and Martha Adams didn't even look up.

Susan spoke even louder, conscious of the buzzing coming from old Mary's large hearing aids. "Mary, the Black Bear?"

"Evening prayer?"

"No, I said the Black Bear. Shall we go?"

"You like Bestow?" The old lady closed her eyes. "Of course. No problem. Bestow onto us, dear Lord Jesus the strength—"

Martha slapped her friend on the arm. "It's your move!"

"Oh goody." The little old lady opened her eyes and lifted her rook.

Susan sighed and reached into her pocket for her phone. She unlocked the screen and scrolled to the third page, tapping on the contacts tab. Surely there would be someone who would enjoy a spot of spur of the moment fun. She moved through her contacts.

Accountant – Carl

China Garden – Chinese

Chiropodist

Danielle Watts – School

Dentist

Doctors

Eden Hairdressers

Jenna James

Marcus Ramsbottom – School

My number

Natalie Jakes

Susan paused. Natalie Jakes. A friend she'd made a couple of months ago at the school Christmas Fayre. Natalie, the daughter of a school governor, had been talked into helping out on the bauble stall, as had Susan. Their friendship had blossomed over a six hour period of selling and wrapping, and numbers were swapped with a pledge to catch up again in the New Year. Susan checked the time, 9.55 p.m., and remembered how Natalie had talked about her new house on the Westbury Homes estate opposite the school. She thought back to the way Natalie had laughed about funny nights out and holidays abroad. Yes, thought Susan, Natalie Jakes was a fun seeking, spur of the moment, type girl. She started to type, trying to sound as cool as she possibly could.

Hey, what's up? How's the start of your year been? Heading over to the Black Bear for a couple of late night drinks now if you fancy it? Sorry, been meaning to catch up for ages, just been hectic, you know how it is!

Susan pressed send and waited.

"Pass the port, please," said Martha, stretching out her hand for the hip flask.

"Sorry, here you go," said Susan, passing it back.

Martha twisted the lid and took a sip. "Are you going to the Black Bear?"

"My evening prayer." Mary nodded. "Let me continue."

"Just turn them off!" shouted Martha, tapping on her own ears and signalling to her friend. She looked back at Susan. "I could do with another bottle of port, please. I tend to whizz up there on my mobility scooter most Sunday mornings, but you could save me a trip. Angel behind the bar knows the one I like. It's called Red Ruby."

Susan nodded. "I'm probably heading off in a bit. Catching up with an old friend." She smiled as her phone beeped. "That'll be her now."

"Have fun!" said Danielle as she stuffed a whole flake into her mouth sideways.

"I will," said Susan, standing up and swiping her phone to life. She read the text on the screen: **Sorry. Who is this? I don't have your number stored.**

Susan's cheeks flared up with colour, for once pleased with the poor lighting in the room.

"Ladies, ladies, ladies! What's the action in here tonight then?" Marcus Ramsbottom was arms up, hanging from the frame of the door. "Nothing's going on in my block."

"Susan's off to the Black Bear," said Danielle through the chocolate.

"Really? Who with? At this time?" Marcus was pulling a face of complete incomprehension.

"Umm, it's a bit late actually, I'm not sure if I quite realised the time."

"Oh my mon amie, have you been stood up?"

"No, I—"

"I'll come with you. Angel's always pleased to see me."

Martha Adams added to the conversation. "Red Ruby. Angel knows the one."

Susan thought about the options. An hour gaining weight with Danielle. An hour in her room obsessing about Jenna. Or an hour at the Black Bear with Marcus. She sighed. At least she'd be able to say she'd been out. "Are we walking?"

"Take my scooter if you like," said Martha.

Marcus snorted. "Angel loves the fact I drive a Punto Sport, there's no way I'm going up on your old lady's mobility scooter."

"Thank you for the offer," added Susan.

"It takes two," said Martha. "Mary here's always straddling the back. We hare right up that school drive in no time. She's always been good with electrics." Martha raised her voice. "Haven't you, Mary?"

Mary cocked her ear. "What?"

"Good with electrics."

"I'm not dyslexic."

"No! You're good with electrics! You've tinkered with the motor on our scooter. You've sorted out our speed."

Mary Llewellyn fiddled with her ears. "Speak up! I think I need new batteries."

Marcus lifted his hands to his mouth and made a loudspeaker. "Don't we wind you up at your age, dear?" He smiled at himself and turned to Susan. "I, on the other hand, am the ultimate Duracell bunny. I've got the strength of a rock."

"Yes, you're a cock," muttered Mary.

Marcus sniffed and turned around, throwing his arm over Susan's shoulder. "Come on, my mon amie. A moonlit walk for the young romantics."

****

Susan stepped closer to the cast iron radiator, warmed by the heat and friendly atmosphere in the old English pub. Marcus was at the bar getting the drinks, and there was a dreadlocked musician playing a ukulele on a makeshift stage. She looked around at the other people in the black and white timber-framed building, all laughing and joking, enjoying each other's company in the cosy, yet quaint, old-world setting. Susan caught sight of a kissing young couple and felt a pang of emotion. No, not tonight, she thought. Tonight she was out. She was out socialising. Socialising on a Saturday night. She smiled to herself. Yes, the ten minute brisk walk in the cold with Marcus's claptrap had been worth it, for the simple reason she'd be able to tell Jenna she had a life. She glanced around the bar, eyes drawn, as always, to the low beams and bumpy wattle and daub walls. The Black Bear was a treasure-trove of trinkets and historical character, and Susan wondered why she didn't spend more time here. It was close. It was welcoming, in a snuggly sort of fashion. She paused her thought as Marcus handed over half a pint of Special Surrey Stout. She thought again. It stocked great local ale. Marcus let out a low belch and chewed something off the corner of his moustache. Susan sighed. She knew the reason why she didn't spend more time here. The reason was simple. She didn't have the friends to accompany her.

"So, mon amie," said Marcus, "what shall we discuss?"

Susan looked towards the stage. "Shall we just listen? He seems rather good."

"He needs a thorough washing with industrial soap if you ask me."

Susan turned back around and looked at Marcus's greasy moustache and lank ginger hair. "Please, Marcus."

"Come on, my mon amie, let's chat. Let's set the world to rights. Let's solve life's biggest problems. Let's ponder the world's greatest questions. Let's—"

Susan sighed. "What would you like to talk about, Marcus?"

"Protocol on a date. The female perspective."

"Oh Marcus," sighed Susan, "this isn't a date."

Marcus sneered. "Oh poor you. How embarrassing. No, sorry to disappoint, but I'm talking about Angel. She's just agreed to come to lunch with me tomorrow and I'd like some guidance on first date protocol." He sniggered to himself. "I realise you won't be much help, but maybe you've read something in one of those trashy magazines of yours."

"I'm dating Jenna," said Susan. "I do have some experience, and I don't read trashy magazines."

"Susan, Susan, Susan, let's discuss this first." Marcus was displaying his best sympathy face. "She's gone. She's had her fun. But now she's gone."

"She's coming back at the end of April."

Marcus shook his head. "No, she's not."

"She's already sent in her School Direct application form."

"Susan, stop. You're making a fool of yourself." He took a deep breath. "Okay, time for some tough love. The chances of Jenna James continuing this charade as your girlfriend as she completes her teaching training here at St Wilfred's are close to zero. The chance of Jenna James remembering how wonderful it is to live the carefree life on the slopes with a multitude of women at her fingertips is almost certainly one hundred percent." He sighed. "Susan, she's had her fun. But now she's gone."

"She's my girlfriend. She's my partner. We're a couple."

Marcus laughed. "Give her a call. She'll be out. It's après ski night every night for instructors like her."

"I know she's out."

"So you know what she'll be up to then."

Susan nodded. "Yes, she'll be socialising with her friends."

"No, she'll be drinking and dancing. She'll be flirting and kissing, and she'll be getting up to whatever it is you lesbians get up to with those king-kong sized cocks of yours."

"Marcus!"

"Actually, on that point, do you think a first date is too early to introduce toys like that? I don't want a worldly woman like Angel to think I'm vanilla." He scrunched up his face. "Is that the word? I'm sure I read something like that in one of those women's magazines at the doctors. Anyway, my point is, if someone like *you* uses toys like *that*, then maybe it *is* the norm. Maybe I do need to move with the times and offer my ladies other additional avenues of stimulation." He grinned. "I've always been told my moustache is tantamount to tickling torture when I'm—"

"Marcus! Stop." Susan took a huge gulp of ale. She swallowed quickly and shook her head. "Fine. First date protocol. Where are you going?"

"Sunday lunch."

"Where?"

Marcus lifted a hand to the black and white walls. "Here."

"But she works here."

"Exactly. She said she'd give me extra gravy."

Susan frowned. "She's working tomorrow?"

"Yes, but when I said I was coming in for Sunday lunch she said she might be able to sit down and chat for a bit."

"So it's not an actual date."

"Yes. I said, *'So it's a date,'* and she smiled."

"Marcus, she's a barmaid, she has to smile."

"Just because you're insecure in your relationship doesn't mean you should project those insecurities elsewhere." Marcus nodded towards the stage. "This music's dreadful. Shall I put some money in the jukebox?"

"Don't be ridiculous, you can't try and drown out the live act."

"I can," said Marcus, rummaging around in his pocket for some change.

Susan grabbed his arm. "Please, come on." She glanced around the room. "Look, that table's free at the back. Shall we sit down?"

Marcus studied the delicate fingers wrapped around his wrist and smiled. "Of course, my mon amie. It does look rather secluded back there."

Susan released her grip and held out her hand for his glass that was empty. "Take a seat. I'll get us another."

"Decisive as well. This is the Susan I love."

Susan tried not to shudder as she made her way to the bar, cursing her own stupidity for scraping the barrel in an attempt to impress Jenna. She paused as an elderly man hobbled in front of her and placed his order first. Why had it been so important to come out? Why had she felt the need to prove she had a social life? What did it matter if she was a habitual hermit? And who was she ultimately trying to impress? Susan sighed to herself, not wanting to admit the truth. Jenna and her were polar opposites. Jenna only had to smile at someone and she gained a new friend for life. She was one of those women who couldn't go anywhere without bumping into someone who knew her. She was naturally charismatic and it was obvious why people wanted to socialise with her at every given opportunity. She was the life and soul of the party. Susan, however, realised that *she* was characterised as awkward, unsociable, and not particularly well liked.

"What's the face for, honey?" asked Angel, leaning over the bar, bust first.

"Sorry, nothing, hi, how are you? Two things, please. Could I pick up Martha Adams' bottle of port? She says she usually collects it on a Sunday. And could I also have two more glasses of the stout ale, please."

The buxom blonde brought her piece of well chewed gum to the front of her mouth and started to grind it on her incisors. "You ain't trying to get your hands on my ginger smoochy pants, are you, honey?"

Susan looked shocked. "Marcus?"

"That's the one. He's a good old catch what with those letters behind his name and his fancy Professor title."

Susan coughed. "Yes, I guess he is. I hear you're having lunch tomorrow."

Angel pushed up a boob and pulled down her dress in one smooth action. "Sure are. Boss will only let me take a twenty minute break though." She batted her eyelashes and leaned forwards, almost spilling her breasts onto the bar. "He even says he'll take me up to that big old school of yours one day. Free, isn't it? For you professors to send your kids there?"

"Well, I don't think it's quite free, but it's heavily discounted."

Angel plumped up her curly blonde hair. "My Tammy and Tanisha would be in their element up there."

"You've got children?"

"I know! I don't look old enough, do I? Anyway, honey, I can't stop and gas all day. Drinks and port." Angel lowered her voice. "Does old Martha want a packet of those big long menthol cigarettes of hers as well? I've had another shipment."

Susan fumbled around in her purse for a twenty pound note. "I'm not sure. I'll let her know. Maybe you could pass them on to Marcus tomorrow?"

"Oh no, honey. We both know how anti-smoking that man is."

Susan paused. Actually she didn't. "Do you, umm, do you two spend a lot of time together?"

Angel pulled the bottle of port from the cabinet under the bar and placed it on the counter. "You do like him, don't you, honey!"

"No, no, I just didn't realise you'd got so close."

Angel smoothed down her tight neon dress. "I'm not that kind of girl, honey. And anyway, I'm taking it slowly with this one. This one's a keeper."

"I'm genuinely pleased for you both. I really do hope it works out."

"Thanks, honey. Tell my mister smoochy pants I'll be over in a bit," said Angel, placing the drinks next to the port.

Susan reached for a tray and lifted the drinks, walking back to the table with her mouth slightly ajar. "She likes you, Marcus. I think she really likes you."

"Angel? Of course she does. They all do." He sniffed and looked at the tray. "No scratchings?"

"Pork scratchings? You didn't ask for any."

Marcus shook his head. "Angel always slips me a packet of scratchings. No doubt a ploy to drop them over here herself."

"Quite possibly," said Susan, settling into her seat.

Marcus used his fingertips to wipe some ale from his moustache. "Actually, there is something I've been meaning to mention."

"Okay," said Susan, never knowing quite what to expect.

"Battle-axe Brown." Marcus narrowed his eyes. "She's called a meeting on Monday. Wants to discuss an alleged complaint."

"What's the complaint?"

"No idea, but that cobwebbed old woman has hated me from the moment I arrived at St Wilfred's." He narrowed his eyes. "I think she may be plotting my downfall."

Susan took a sip of her drink. "Why? What on earth would be her motive?"

Marcus lowered his voice. "I rejected her once. Sexually. She couldn't handle it."

Susan almost spluttered. "That's not true."

"It is. I was a new whippersnapper at the school and she asked me if I'd accompany her to her lawn bowls tournament. I politely declined saying I was far too young for her advances, and that was it. My fate was sealed."

Susan shook her head. "What about the assembly? You upset her once, didn't you?"

"That was years ago! And anyway, wouldn't you want to know if there was something on your chin?"

"Yes, but—"

Marcus tutted. "She was in assembly. She was standing at the front. She was about to start, and I noticed she had something on her chin." He shrugged. "So I told her."

"How did you tell her?"

"I was at the side of the hall and I just said, *'Excuse me Vice Principal Brown, you seem to have something on your chin'.*" Marcus shrugged. "She started wiping, so I said, *'No, third one down.'*"

"Oh Marcus."

"But it wasn't that. It was the fact I rejected her." He smoothed down the sides of his moustache. "But it's crossed my mind that I'm her final vendetta. She's got nothing to lose. She's leaving. Maybe she wants to pull me down with her."

"Have you done anything wrong? Is there any truth in the complaint?"

Marcus gasped. "Susan! Mon amie! You know me. I'm the definition of professionalism." He shook his head. "She's just trying to ruffle some feathers before she goes. I know I can count on you to be a character witness though."

Susan bit the inside of her lip. "Actually, Marcus, I've been asked to write—"

"Scratchy, scratchy, scratchy." Angel was seductively dangling a packet of pork scratchings between her breasts. "I'm on a break. Shall we share?"

Marcus snarled. "Only if you feed me, Angel."

"Stick that tongue out then, you bad boy."

Susan coughed. "Should I look for another chair?"

Marcus momentarily allowed his eyes to move from Angel's breasts. "Don't be a trike, Susan."

"A trike?"

He lowered his voice. "The third wheel. The fourth beat of a waltz. The gooseberry fool." He nodded towards the bar. "There's a spare stool over there. A little space wouldn't go amiss."

Susan looked at her glass of stout. "Right, sorry, I'll take this with me," she said, feeling herself flare up with colour.

"We might be a while," said Marcus, sticking out his yellow tongue and flicking it upwards, signalling for Angel to start.

"Right, sorry, I'll just…" Susan stepped away from the feeding frenzy and looked around the room. Maybe she should just go home. Maybe she should— Natalie! Susan burst into a smile as she spotted Natalie Jakes standing on her tiptoes next to the jukebox. "Natalie!" she shouted far too eagerly.

The lady turned around and looked at Susan with zero recognition.

"Natalie! It's Susan!"

The lady continued to look blank.

"From the school! The Christmas Fayre. The baubles!"

"The fayre?" The lady paused. "The fayre, the fayre, the fayre? Oh yes, I think I remember now. Sorry, what was your name again?"

Susan blushed. "Susan … from the fayre … the school fayre."

Natalie Jakes lifted herself back onto her tiptoes and continued her scanning of the room. "Oh right, yes I remember you now. You were wearing a Christmas jumper. A reindeer wasn't it? Anyway, you won't believe this, but I'm here with a couple of friends on a stalking stake out mission." Natalie wafted her long nails. "We were having a girly get together at mine, you know the sort, wine, nail polish, the odd jab of Botox. Anyway I get a strange message asking me to come for a drink. No clue of the sender, and no reply when I asked for their name." She laughed. "We thought it would be a bit of a giggle. Gloria and Jasmine are sneaking around trying to sniff out the weirdo!"

Susan finished her drink in one mouthful and laughed loudly. "How strange! Well, my taxi's waiting. There's a whole gang of us. We're off clubbing. I thought I recognised you, so I quickly dashed over, but they'll be cursing me for holding them up. Giggly girls on a night out, you know how it is!"

"Have fun, Sophie," said Natalie, already back on her tiptoes.
"It's Susan," whispered Susan, slipping silently out of the bar.

CHAPTER EIGHT

Susan let the cold air hit her hard. She kept her jacket unzipped and inhaled sharply as it flapped around her waist. The temperature was low, but nothing could cool the burning fire she felt in her cheeks or the raging humiliation she felt in her heart. She was embarrassed, demeaned, but most of all, she felt worthless. Susan gasped as she threw her head backwards and stared at the stars, feeling as if the whole world was spinning around her. She couldn't focus. What had just happened? Marcus had told her to do one. Marcus! How utterly mortifying. Marcus Ramsbottom had more of a life than she did. She gasped again. The woman she'd spent a full day with only a couple of months ago had forgotten her completely. The woman was searching for a weirdo. A weirdo with no friends.

Susan dropped her head back down and resumed her walk, picking up her pace towards the large iron gates that were now closed over the main entrance to St Wilfred's All-Girls School. She fumbled in her pockets for her bunch of keys and found the one that would unlock the old-fashioned padlock that was securing the chain around the main gates. It was the only thing stopping intruders from entering the school grounds and could easily be cut off if anyone so wished. She pulled it open and pushed through, closing the gates quickly behind her and reattaching the lock. She stepped into the shadows and leaned backwards against the old stone wall that protected the grounds. The grounds where she'd always felt so safe, so normal, and so at home. Who was she trying to kid? She wasn't a party animal like Jenna. She was an academic, and academics spent their Saturday nights reading, or watching documentaries, or socialising with other academics in a communal, albeit fusty, lounge.

Susan reached into her jacket pocket and took out her phone. She swiped it to life and clicked on the green dial button, seeing Jenna's name flash up as her most recent contact. She tapped the screen and stepped back onto the path. The idea that Marcus may have followed her out of the pub and could potentially hear the call was one embarrassment too many. She looked over her shoulder into the darkness. Of course he hadn't followed her out. He had a life. Marcus Ramsbottom had a—

Susan stopped her obsessing as she heard the international dial tone. She knew Jenna wouldn't answer, but she needed to feel close to her all the same. It rang six times before the answerphone kicked in.

"Hey, you're through to Jenna's phone. Leave me a message, please."

Susan wasn't prepared for the tears that started to well up at the back of her eyes, and she certainly wasn't prepared for the way her voice started to crack as she spoke.

"J-Jenna, hey, it's, it's me. I, umm, I miss you." She paused, trying to control her emotions. "Sorry, I'm fine. I'm fine. I just wanted to leave you a message." Susan bit her bottom lip as she held back the tears. "Actually I'm not fine. I'm alone. I'm walking back to the school and I, umm, I wanted some company. I've been to the Black Bear with Marcus." She paused. "I know what you're thinking. What am I doing going to the Black Bear with Marcus, and if I'm honest I don't know either. I was…" She paused. "Umm, I was trying to impress you I think. How stupid does that sound? It's just, it's just that I don't want you worrying about me. I don't want you worrying that I haven't got any friends." Susan sniffed back a tear. "But I don't think I have." She pulled the phone away from her ear as she let out a heartfelt sob. "Sorry, this is ridiculous. I'm going to call you back."

Susan paused her walk and shook her head, desperately trying to pull herself together. The last thing Jenna needed to hear was her falling apart. She pressed the redial button and waited for the tone. She spoke louder and with more confidence. "Sorry, right, ignore that last message please. I'm fine. I've just had a bit of a strange evening. I wanted to do something. I wanted to show you I had a life, so I tried to get someone to come to the pub with me, but no one would." She laughed to herself. "I know I haven't really got rich pickings up at the school, but I thought someone might want a quick drink. Hey, I even texted a woman I met recently, trying to act all casual about nipping for a drink, but she didn't even have my number stored. She didn't even know who I was." Susan paused as she felt the tears returning. "I, umm, I guess I wanted to show you that I'm going to be fine. I wanted to show you that I wouldn't be sitting in my room every evening, obsessing about what you're getting up to." Susan gasped at herself.

"But look at me. I'm calling you in tears instead. I'm sorry. I'm useless at this. Is there a way I can delete my messages?" Susan pulled the phone away from her ear and looked at the screen, pressing the red end button by mistake.

"Sorry," she said, having redialled and connected once more. "I ended the call. You're going to get these messages, aren't you? You're going to hear me stuttering away like a lunatic." Susan took a deep breath. "I love you. I really love you, Jenna. You've changed my world. You've changed me. I'm a different person when I'm with you. I'm confident. I'm carefree." She paused. "I have a life. We do things. We have adventures. We're a team. I don't worry about anything when I'm with you. I know it sounds completely cheesy but it's true. You complete me." Susan laughed to herself. "Now you're cringing as you listen to this, aren't you? But it's true. You're my missing piece, Jenna. You're the person who brings out the best in me. The person who makes me make sense, if that makes sense? Oh listen to me, I'm as rubbish with words as you are. I guess I'm just trying to tell you that I love you. I love you so much. And yes I'm worried. I'm worried that it's day one and I'm acting like this. I want to be the person you want. The person you fell for. But you've only ever seen me around you, and around you I'm different. Now it's just me, and this is me. Friendless. Bumbling. Somewhat dramatic." Susan laughed. "Listen to me. What a catch! I guess I just tried to play it cool tonight. I tried to be the person I thought you wanted me to be. But I'm not that person, Jenna. I'd rather just wait for you to come back and let you reignite whatever it is that you ignite in me. That fire. That drive. That sense of adventure. I guess I don't have it when you're not around. Look at me. I'm back to the Susan I was before."

Susan sighed to herself and ended the call, squeezing the phone tightly and throwing her head backwards. "What am I doing?" she shouted to the stars.

"Anything I can help with?" said the voice in the darkness.

"Bob? Is that you?" Susan squinted her eyes and looked in the direction of the large round patch of soil.

"Bloody Daisy Button and her crutch! She managed to poke everything out of place. Everything out of place I say. And my Timmy wasn't much better. I've had to dig the bulbs up and start again." Bob was using the pitchfork to help him down the small hill. "These youngsters don't understand the importance of timing. If I don't get it sorted tonight we might not get the blooming come spring."

Susan smiled. "You always get the best blooming come spring."

"Yes, because of the timings." He stepped onto the path and stretched out his back. "Anyway, I'm almost done. Almost done I say." He lowered his voice. "Saw you walking past with that Professor Ramsbottom earlier. Stayed quiet, didn't I."

"Oh Bob, you could have joined us. We only went for a quick drink at the Black Bear. You must be freezing out here."

"Pffft! No chance you'd get me sharing a pint with that plonker."

"Bob!"

"What? He is, and I, err, I noticed him getting into your car earlier too." Bob bowed his head slightly. "Don't think I'm talking out of turn, Madam Quinn, but I do hope you're not starting something up now that lovely young lady of yours has moved on."

"No! He's a friend."

Bob looked puzzled. "Really? I thought you'd keep better company."

Susan shook her head. "Marcus is fine. He was doing me a favour actually. I wanted someone to come out with me."

"Be careful, Madam Quinn. He's the type of man who calls in favours. Calls in favours I say."

Susan rubbed her arms and shivered at the preposterousness of the situation. A midnight warning on the dark school driveway from an old man who smelled strongly of peat. She glanced at her watch. Well, it was 10.55 p.m. and Bob was hardly a stranger, but still. "I need to head back. I'm cold. Are you coming?"

Bob shook his head. "No, I've got another twenty minutes at least."

"You're the hardest working groundsman I know."

Bob scratched his grey sideburns. "Know many groundsmen do you?"

"I don't know many anybodys, Bob. That's exactly my problem."

****

Susan reached out from her duvet and felt for her phone. She drew it back into her warm den and swiped it to life, immediately blinded by the glaring light. She slowly opened one eye and squinted at the screen. The green message box in the top left hand corner was still green. No red circle with a number in it, telling her she had a message. Just a green box with an empty white speech bubble, telling her that no one wanted to talk. She looked at the time: 3.55 a.m. It had taken great restraint to avoid calling Jenna again. Three rambling messages were more than enough for anyone to come home to, and her simple text message of: **Please call me before you listen to your voicemails** had obviously not worked.

Susan lay still and weighed up her options. She could, A, do nothing and spend the remainder of her sleep time checking and re-checking her phone. She could, B, text again and hope that Jenna was in the mood to answer. Or she could, C, call. She could call and get the earful that was no doubt heading her way out in the open, sooner rather than later. Susan pressed the green redial button and waited. Every single beep of the international dial tone felt like forever. She tried to avoid counting them in her head but knew on the sixth one that Jenna wasn't answering. "Hey," she said, trying not to sound too groggy, "you always sleep with your phone on loud, so I'm assuming you don't want to talk to me, and you're well within your rights to take that course of action. I'm sorry, Jenna. I'm really sorry for the way I've been this evening. I bet you think I've totally fallen apart over here, and I guess if I'm honest I have." Susan paused. "You, umm, you did promise me though that you'd text when you got in, but I'm guessing you listened to all of my warbling messages and threw your phone down in disgust."

Susan shook her head at herself. "I just don't know how to make this better. I guess you need some space, don't you? Space from me and my neediness. I've really shown myself up tonight and I'm sorry. I would love to talk but I understand that it has to be when you're ready. It has to be on your terms. So I'm going to put my phone down and roll over and try and get some sleep. I've got a pretty easy day tomorrow, just catching up on a bit of marking, so call me, or text me, or email me, or whatever's easiest, and only when you're ready. I'm a total loser, Jenna, and I'm sorry. I'm sorry for all of this. You deserve better, so…" Susan closed her eyes and pressed her head further into her pillow. "I just never thought I'd have someone like you in my life, and now you're not in my life I'm not quite sure what I'm supposed to do. I don't like feeling like this. I don't like scraping the barrel for people to socialise with. But I don't want to be the person I was. You've shown me how to live, Jenna, and now that you're not here I feel like I'm dying." Susan screwed up her face as she heard herself say it. "Sorry, the dramatics have returned. I'm going. I'm rolling over. I'll talk to you tomorrow … maybe … hopefully. Bye."

Susan placed her phone back on her bedside table and cringed at herself in absolute despair.

CHAPTER NINE

Jenna woke up with a start at the sound of the loud chalet bell. It was the warning signal that gave the instructors half an hour to get up and out. Sunday was always busy on the slopes with new arrivals eager to get out and about for their first full day of skiing. All of the reps in the chalet were required to meet their new groups in the ski garden at 10.00 a.m. sharp to assess their requirements for the week ahead. Jenna actually preferred looking after the school groups, even though the pickups started on a Saturday at the services. Plus there was the whole element of evening entertainment to sort out as well, but she preferred them for one main reason: The hangovers weren't usually as bad. Staying in the chalet was dangerous. It was far too easy to get talked into going out every night and crawling in every morning. When she was at Sylvie's, looking after a school, she got to drink, chat, and socialise without a group of raucous reps shoving the latest beer funnel or bottle bong down her neck.

Jenna stretched out her arms and yawned. At least this small group of execs only needed her from 10.00 a.m. till 4.00 p.m., and from their requirements sheet it had looked like they were all pretty competent skiers, simply wanting a guide for the week. Jenna smiled. She'd be able to get some great skiing in too.

"Up and out!" came the shout, accompanied by a loud fist banging on the door.

"Moving," she shouted back, completely understanding why they needed such draconian measures in the chalets. The average age of a Club Ski instructor was twenty five, and the average relationship status was single, hence the wild nights out and difficult early morning get ups. Jenna threw her legs out of the bed and stood up, knowing the best course of action was an immediate shower. If she wasn't out in the communal area within fifteen minutes the chalet supervisor would enter her room with his key and black mark her. Three black marks in one week and she'd be reported.

She stretched again, lifting herself onto her tiptoes and rolling her neck, almost giving herself whiplash as she suddenly swung her head towards the phone that lay silently on her bedside cabinet. "Susan!" she gasped, realising she'd forgotten to text once she'd got in. In fact she'd deliberately decided not to take her phone out with her to avoid that huge temptation to call and whisper sweet nothings all evening, no doubt annoying Susan, as well as the friends she was supposed to be partying with. She'd had it all planned. A quick drink with the reps and a continuation of FaceTime fun and frolics with Susan. It hadn't, however, quite worked out like that.

Jenna jumped back onto the bed and grabbed the phone, cursing her own stupidity. She'd fallen into that all too easy Saturday night ski rep habit of going out at 10.00 p.m. and crawling in at 5.00 a.m. Seven hours of drinking and dares. Seven hours of stupidity. She scrunched her face into her hands, not daring to bring the phone to life. Jenna rubbed her temples, trying really hard to remember. Visions of drinking games flashed through her mind, and the image of a drunken dance-off in the kebab shop to some strange Turkish music kept reappearing. She thought harder. Annie and Dave had announced their engagement. That's why she'd stayed out, wasn't it? To celebrate the coupling that no one believed would last.

Jenna shook her head. She'd been good though, hadn't she? She thought carefully and nodded, vaguely remembering seeing Amber straddling Sid the snowplough driver. Yes, thought Jenna with more certainty, she'd been good. But how had she got home? She couldn't even remember getting into bed, let alone looking at her phone to check for messages, or sending the 'I'm safe' text that Susan would so desperately have wanted. She swiped the screen to life. Four voicemails and seven texts. "Bugger," she said to herself, quite unsure what to do.

"Are we moving in there? I heard it was a late one." Steve, the chalet supervisor was banging once more.

"I'm moving. Don't worry. I'm moving."

"It's always harder to get into the swing of it after a week off. You're one of our best, Jenna. Don't let me down."

"I'm moving, Steve. I'm showering right now." Jenna placed the phone down on the cabinet and stood back up, swaying slightly as she held her head, wondering how on earth she was going to make it up to Susan. She walked into her tiny bathroom and leaned into the shower cubicle, turning up the heat before taking off her underwear and stepping under the spray. She sighed to herself. She didn't want to check her messages yet as she wasn't properly prepared for the guilt they'd no doubt induce. Jenna reached for the three-in-one shower wash and hastily squeezed it into the palm of her hand, rubbing it all over her body, and using more for her hair. Poor Susan, she thought, as the lather started to build. She'd have spent all night worrying about her whereabouts. Probably assuming she was shacked up with Amber, no doubt. And who could blame her? Their first evening apart and she hadn't managed to do the one thing she'd promised to do. "You idiot!" shouted Jenna, throwing her head backwards under the water.

Jenna jumped out of the shower and towel dried her hair as frantically as she could, managing to add blasts from the hairdryer as she threw on her salopettes and red Club Ski Jacket.

"Five minute warning," came the shout and latest bang.

Jenna kept the hairdryer on, lying it down on the dresser and angling the nozzle towards her as she bent down to pull on her thick ski socks. She shook her head, hoping her mass of brown locks would continue to dry. There was nothing worse than hitting the slopes with wet hair, as it almost guaranteed the onset of one of those cold, pounding headaches. She grabbed her Moon Boots from under the dresser and thrust her feet inside, lifting the hairdryer back up and blasting away as quickly as she could. She thought through her plan. She'd slap on some moisturising sun cream and grab a coffee from the communal area, which she'd drink en route to the ski garden. Yes, she thought, she'd be fine. In fact there was nothing better than a long ski in the crisp fresh air to sort out a hangover like this. She shook her hair one final time, pleased with the level of dryness, and reached out for her phone. She'd call Susan and offer apology after apology after apology whilst filling her jacket with the essentials - ski pass, cash, sunblock, gloves, Club Ski pager, sunglasses and hip flask. She shook her head. She'd leave the hip flask at home today.

Jenna lifted the phone and started the multitasking, ignoring the messages and voicemails and scrolling straight to Susan's number instead. She stuffed her gloves into her pockets as she clicked on Susan's name, but watched in horror as the phone momentarily flashed a white empty battery symbol at her before shutting itself down completely. "NO!" gasped Jenna, shaking the screen as if it might miraculously come back to life. She grabbed her final few essentials and threw the phone down onto the bed, racing as quickly as she could from her room.

"I don't know how you do it, Jenna," said Steve. "You drink like a fish in the evening, but look like a swan in the morning."

"Steve, my phone's dead. Can I take a Club Ski one please?"

"Sure, no problem," said Steve, quickly avoiding the embarrassment of having another compliment fall on deaf ears. "Do you need a pager too?"

"No, I've got mine, thanks." Jenna stood still and waited.

"Oh, sorry, I've not got them on me. I've given them to Lisa. She's already down at the ski gard—"

"Thanks," shouted Jenna, pushing out of the double doors and crossing the hall to the heated boot room. She stepped inside and pulled her heavy Rossignol ski boots from the shelf in the corner, sitting down on the bench and kicking her feet free from the padded Moon Boots, shoving them into the firm plastic instead. She tightened the buckles and clipped them closed, grabbing her skis and poles from the rack as she left. The sun almost blinded her as she stepped out onto the crunchy snow, but she managed to drop her skis and pull out her glasses without wincing too much. She pushed the glasses onto her nose and fixed the ends under her ski hat, stepping into her bindings and tightening her scarf like a pro. It was one of those mornings that was bright, yet cold, and Jenna knew the weather had the ability to go either way. You could be skiing the slopes in a short-sleeved vest one minute, and wrapped up the next. She stabbed her poles into the white ice and pushed off quickly, heading down the small slope towards the ski garden. She skied straight, standing tall and breathing in the crisp fresh air. She had plenty of time before her lesson, but what she really needed was time with Susan. Time to make this right.

"Wowzers, Jenna! You're the first one here. I certainly didn't expect that after last night!" Club Ski instructor Lisa was laying out piles of fluorescent vests for the groups of young children expected to arrive in the next twenty minutes or so.

"Please tell me I behaved?" Jenna used her poles to unclip the back of her bindings and step down onto the snow.

"Behave? You?" Lisa laughed. "Oh bless you, you have no idea do you?"

Jenna felt a surge of panic well up in her stomach. "What did I do?"

Lisa dropped the vests and reached out to rub the sides of Jenna's arms. "You spent the whole evening like a love struck puppy telling everyone how happy you were. How you'd met the woman of your dreams. How you were going to marry her by Christmas."

"Stop it!"

"You did!" said Lisa, laughing. "Bless you, Jenna, you were so sweet. But you did keep trying to sneak home, so I think they started giving you doubles."

"That's why I can't remember anything!"

"You make the party, Jenna. You're the fun-est friend we've got."

"Can you tell that to Susan?"

Lisa frowned. "That you're fun? I'm sure she knows that already."

"No! That I was talking about her all night and that I got my drinks spiked."

"I'm not sure they were quite spiked. By midnight you were lining up the shots all by yourself."

"Please Lisa, I'm in the dog house. I forgot to text when I got in. She'll be really worried. I feel absolutely dreadful."

Lisa laughed. "Get her on the line then."

"No, that's just it, my phone's dead. I'll have to take one of the Club Ski ones out today."

Lisa reached down into the large red back pack and pulled out an old-fashioned Nokia. "Charged and ready to go. You want me to dial her for you, Romeo? Your hands are shaking a bit."

"Sure," said Jenna. "The number's…" Jenna closed her eyes as a shiver of emptiness washed through her. "Oh bugger," she said, with a groan.

CHAPTER TEN

Susan looked up from her marking and stared out of the large window that overlooked the acre in front of the school. She was sitting at one of the modern workstations in the old-fashioned library, still cross that the governors hadn't managed to adapt the longstanding wooden desks, choosing instead to rip them all out and replace them with these workstations that were more suited to modern office blocks. Susan stretched her neck and looked up at the rows of tall bookshelves overflowing with novels, journals, reference books, and encyclopaedias. She couldn't remember the last time she'd seen a student up a ladder. They were obviously too busy plugging their laptops, tablets, and other electrical devices into these new sockets on these new workstations.

Susan sighed to herself. She must be getting old. She checked her watch again. 3.00 p.m., that would make it 4.00 p.m. in Morzine. She wasn't getting old. It was simply her bad mood making her cynical. The same bad mood that was making her comments harsher than usual on the Year Ten general studies papers she was marking. The bad mood that had suppressed her appetite at breakfast and lunch. The bad mood that was completely self-inflicted. Caused by her own stupidity and inability to act cool. Jenna was right to give her some breathing space. No one wanted a wailing banshee for a girlfriend.

Susan closed her eyes and thought of a plan of action. She could wait until Jenna calmed down. But what if Jenna never calmed down? What if she never heard from Jenna ever again? Susan kept her eyes closed and shook her head. No, she would have to make the first move. But what could she do? Phoning was a definite no. Sending a text was a definite no. Maybe she'd email. Susan nodded. Yes, an email that was calm, thoughtful, and apologetic. That would work, wouldn't it? Susan shook her head. No, Jenna would probably delete it before reading.

"Madam Quinn, are you having a fit?" Priggy Bunton-Chatsworth was crouching down and peering closely at her teacher's closed eyes and shaking head.

"Of course she's not having a fit, Priggs." Champagne Willington bent down next to her friend. "You're not having a fit are you, Susie?"

Susan opened both eyes and immediately moved backwards in her chair. "Why are you two so close?" She blinked a couple of times. "And Champagne, I'd like it if you could refrain from calling me Susie now that we're back in school."

"Oh no," said Champagne, huffing, "Jenna's gone and you're turning back into the old version of you."

"I like both versions of you, Madam Quinn," said Priggy, maintaining her eye contact.

"I don't have two versions, girls. I'd just like to reinstill that appropriate level of respect now we're back in school."

"We respected you on the ski trip," said Champagne. "We respected your cool clothes, your cool girlfriend, your—"

"Stop please, Champagne."

Champagne pulled up a chair and sat down. "Are you upset?"

"I'm upset that my Year Ten general studies classes haven't applied themselves in this latest essay."

Priggy pulled up a seat on the other side of her teacher and placed a hand on her shoulder. "Champs didn't mean that."

Susan coughed uncomfortably and tried to shake herself free. "Girls. Our ski trip was wonderful, but now we're back in school you need to remember the boundaries. We all need to knuckle down and focus on the job at hand. You have your exams around the corner, and I have to make sure all of my classes are up to speed."

"She's upset, Priggs."

"I know she is, Champs."

"Girls, I'm not upset."

"Was it the photos?" asked Champagne. "It must be hard seeing her having all that fun while you're here all alone with your marking."

"What fun?"

"The party last night." Champagne laughed. "Hugo puts the funniest captions on his posts."

"What posts? What party?"

Champagne and Priggy shared a nervous glance. "You're on Facebook, aren't you?"

"No, why? Is Jenna?"

Champagne failed to hold back a giggle. "She was last night."

Priggy giggled too. "All over it."

"That one on the bar!" Champagne was laughing now. "What was Hugo's caption?"

Priggy was holding her nose and snorting back the giggles. "Tequila covered tits—"

"—and I still prefer todgers," finished off Champagne.

Susan wasn't laughing. "Who had tequila covered? What did you say?"

"Umm," Champagne took hold of herself. "No, Hugo just posted some pictures."

"Hugo the ski rep?"

"Yes," nodded Champagne.

Susan was frowning. "You're friends with Hugo?"

"Yes, I added him. I added Lisa, too."

Priggy smiled. "I even added old Sylvie from the guest house, but she doesn't post much apart from French food recipes." She scrunched up her nose. "I might delete her."

"We're friends with Amber too," said Champagne. "Remember her with the pink hair? She was looking after Mossyside Comp and Mischa and Phats."

"Amber?" Susan glanced down at the phone Champagne had been clutching the whole time. "May I, umm, may I see?"

"My friends list?"

"No, the photos."

"Just add me. I'll send them through. We need to go. We were only cutting through the library to get out onto the acre."

"I'm not on Facebook." Susan tried to sound casual. "It won't take a minute will it?"

Champagne stood back up and returned her chair to the workstation. "Sorry, we're Skyping Mischa and Phats from the front of the school."

Priggy nodded. "They said they wanted to see our hood, to see how different it was to theirs up in Manchester. We thought a Skype from the bottom of the acre with the school in the background would work best."

Champagne tapped her phone. "We can come back up afterwards if you like though. Or we can show you in class tomorrow?"

"No, no, it's fine."

Champagne patted her teacher's shoulder. "Keep smiling, Susie. She'll be back before you know it. And we'll let you use our phone to spy on her in the meantime if that's what you really want."

"Bye Madam Quinn," said Priggy.

"No, I don't ..." Susan tailed off as the girls disappeared around one of the tall bookshelves. "I, umm ..." Susan dropped her eyes to her papers. "I, umm ..." She shook her head and whispered to herself. "Tequila covered tits?"

****

Jenna waved goodbye to her group of execs and slid through the snow to the brightly coloured ski garden. The day had actually been great fun, and her small group, consisting of three middle-aged men and one twenty-something woman, were all amiable and well-motivated, not to mention confident skiers, which meant they were able to cover nearly all of the slopes from the Chamossiere area over to La Rosta. The views of Mont Blanc had been incredible and for a split second Jenna had been able to forget about her current excruciating situation. But it was literally just that, a split second, before her stomach plunged again and she remembered the horror of her mess. Susan must be in such a panic, wondering what on earth had happened to her and why she hadn't called.

Jenna pulled the crappy black Nokia from her pocket and slid to a stop at the small white picket fence that surrounded one side of the ski garden where masses of tiny toddlers were slowly shuffling around in a line. She signalled to Lisa who was pointing the leader of the line in the direction of a small slope and a giant red animal that looked like a cross between a fox and a squirrel. The toddlers started to pick up speed before whizzing into the creature's bottom and out of its front with giggles and whoops of laughter.

Lisa acknowledged Jenna's waving hand and sent the line off towards the magic carpet before skiing quickly to the fence. "How's the head?"

"The head's fine," said Jenna, "but the heart's broken."

"Oh stop it you softy. Did you manage to get through?"

Jenna handed the phone over. "No. This bloody thing doesn't have the internet, and it won't let us dial premium 118 numbers. I was going to Google the school's number and see if I could contact Susan that way."

Lisa glanced back at her group, all still shunting their way up the small slope on the flat escalator. "What about lunch? Why didn't you head down into the village and nip to that internet café?"

"My skiers were too good. We ended up staying near the top. We ate at La Rosta and you can hardly get a phone signal up there, let alone 3G."

"Didn't any of your execs have a phone you could borrow?"

"Lisa! I tried all this. Don't make me feel bad for not trying."

"I'm not."

"They're all 'de-stressing' apparently. They're bankers for some top firm and have agreed on a phone-free week."

Lisa smiled. "I bet that lady slips you her number."

"What lady? Jade? No. She's not interested." Jenna shook the image of the pretty blonde out of her mind. "*I'm* not interested. I love Susan and I've got some huge making up to do."

"Get out of here then," said Lisa, pointing up the slope towards the ski rep chalet.

Jenna used her poles to unclip her skis and stepped down onto the snow that was now really slushy. "I'll walk up. I need some time to plan my response."

"You've had all day to plan your response."

"No, I've had all day to panic."

"And look at Jade."

"No!"

"Come on, Jenna, you can't tell me you haven't enjoyed spending the past six hours in the company of that blue-eyed beauty. I'm straight but I spotted her."

"Why do people always do that?"

"Do what?"

"Add in the fact they're straight when they compliment someone of the same sex."

Lisa sucked on her lips. "I was doing more than compliment. She's hot. I mean seriously hot. Those lips are to die for, and their colour, they're just so perfectly pink."

Jenna nodded. "I couldn't work out if they had some sort of stain on them or if they were naturally that—" She stopped herself. "What am I doing? I'm going. I'll see you tomorrow." Jenna reached down and picked up her skis, clipping them together and lifting them onto her shoulder.

"You'll see me tonight. It's Shot-Sunday down at Maimie's."

"I'm giving it a miss," said Jenna.

"See you at Shot-Sunday," shouted Lisa, turning back around and re-joining her group.

Jenna started her hike up the hill, slamming the tips of her boots into the snow for extra support. The temperature was dropping and she could feel the chill on her cheeks. She exhaled heavily and thought of her plan of action. She'd drop her ski gear off in the boot room and dash back to her bedroom to plug in her phone. She'd take a quick shower whilst it was charging, before throwing on some comfy clothes and settling down on the bed for the make or break phone call. Jenna nodded to herself. Everything would be fine. Susan would understand.

CHAPTER ELEVEN

Susan dumped her general studies exam papers on the worktop in the centre of her small apartment. She hadn't been able to concentrate in the library and knew what she had to do. She had to see the photos. One way or another she *had* to see them. What if Jenna had got so drunk that she had ended up in A&E? What if she had slipped from some bar and was now trapped, locked in until opening time this evening? Susan reached down and picked up her laptop bag. She lifted it to the counter and quickly removed its contents. They must be mistaken. Jenna wouldn't pose for pictures. Not those sort of pictures anyway. She paused her thought as the screen lit up, and clicked on Google Chrome. Within seconds she was typing www.facebook.com into the browser. She thought it best to start all over again so she entered her name and email address into the sign up box. She confirmed her password as StWilfreds, the same as all of her other passwords, added her birthday and clicked on the *female* button. Susan held her breath and signed up, only to be told her email address was already in use. She rolled her eyes and thought back to when she'd first joined, vaguely remembering it was during her PGCE year here at St Wilf's under mounting pressure from the other PGCE student, Barbara Hooty. Barbara hadn't lasted a term, probably due to the influence of Facebook, thought Susan, re-entering her email address into the members sign in section instead. She closed her eyes and thought what her password might have been. Let's try StWilfreds, she thought, entering the text and immediately accessing the account that had been inactive for the past six years.

Susan gasped in horror at the profile picture staring back at her. She was six years younger with a pudding basin haircut and a sprinkling of spots. Susan peered in closer, wondering what on earth that badger jumper was all about. Crikey, she thought, clicking on the home button and seeing the timeline flash up, why were all of her old posts showing up? Susan scrolled down. Actually there were only three. The first said:

71

Hi Facebook, I'm new. The second said: **Still figuring this out.** The third said: **Not a clue what I'm doing, someone help me please.** Not one of the posts had been liked or commented on.

Susan scrolled up to the *friends* button and clicked on the link. The one friend she had had, whom she assumed was Barbara Hooty, had deserted her, and now she was all alone. *Stop it*, she said to herself, mind back on the task at hand. She moved the cursor to the white search box at the top and entered Champagne Willington's name. One result flashed up, and from the small jpeg of hair and pout Susan knew it was St Wilfred's very own J-Lo look-alike. She clicked on the profile. Nothing was visible on Champagne's timeline apart from a green *add friend* button. She didn't want to do that, so she clicked on Champagne's friends list instead. Again nothing was visible. *"Drat,"* said Susan under her breath. She tried Priggy Bunton-Chatsworth. One result flashed up, and from the slightly plump face and cheeky grin it was obviously the one and only Priggs, as Champagne so lovingly called her.

Susan clicked on Priggy's timeline, surprised when a stream of photos and updates appeared. There were screen shots of Priggy's Skypes with Mischa, and lots of rainbow themed posters declaring her love for life and her love for lesbians. Susan continued to scroll, feeling incredibly embarrassed that she was able to see such personal posts. She looked at the small grey globe that kept appearing and moved her cursor over it. A box flashed up saying: **Shared with: Public.** *Wow,* thought Susan, *so anyone can see this?* She clicked on Priggy's friends list and felt her heart quicken when she realised they were all visible. She moved to the search friends box and typed in Hugo's name. Two results flashed up. Hugo Bunton-Chatsworth, possibly an uncle or much older brother, and Hugo Fabian, the ski instructor they'd all met two weeks ago. Susan clicked on the smiling jpeg, holding her breath in preparation for the tequila tit shot. "Damn," she said as the screen went blank with nothing visible apart from the green add friend button. Susan dropped her face into her hands. "What am I doing?" she cried.

****

Jenna settled herself down onto her bed. She was showered, warm, and ready to face the music. She lifted her phone and noticed the voicemail symbol. Jenna thought carefully. Did she want a heads up about the true level of Susan's anger, or would she rather just call and get the ear bashing over with? Her finger hovered over the screen, unsure of her preference. Yep, she thought, pressing the voicemail button. Better to know where Susan was at.

Jenna leaned back on the pillow and pulled her knees into her chest, listening to the staccato voice telling her she had four new messages.

"**10.45 p.m. Saturday 22nd February:** J-Jenna, hey, it's, it's me. I, umm, I miss you."

Jenna sat up, shocked at the way Susan's voice was wobbling. She turned up the volume and pressed the phone harder into her ear. Susan was sniffing back a tear and telling her she didn't have any friends. There was a cough and an abrupt end to the call. "*Shit*," said Jenna, inhaling nervously.

"**10.49 p.m. Saturday 22nd February:** Sorry, right, ignore that last message please. I'm fine."

Jenna nodded and relaxed momentarily before freezing once again as Susan started to cry and tell her she had no friends. "*Susan, what are you doing?*" gasped Jenna, moving on to the third message.

"**10.51 p.m. Saturday 22nd February:** Sorry I ended the call. You're going to get these messages, aren't you? You're going to hear me stuttering away like a lunatic."

"*Yes, I am,*" said Jenna in total shock, wincing as she heard Susan call herself friendless, bumbling and somewhat dramatic. Jenna shook her head. She had been expecting a flood of angry voicemails chastising her for forgetting to call, accusing her of messing around, or getting too drunk, but not this. This actually seemed a little bit worse. Susan was falling apart.

"**3.55 a.m.:** Hey, you always sleep with your phone on loud, so I'm assuming you don't want to talk to me, and you're well within your rights to take that course of action."

Jenna shook her head. *It was 4.55 a.m. over here. I wasn't even in yet! I didn't take my phone out!* She closed her eyes and dropped her head back down to the pillow as she heard Susan taking her last breath and declaring she was dying. "Fuck," said Jenna ending the call and dropping the phone onto the bed. "Fuck, fuck, fuck, fuck, fuck." Susan thought she was ignoring her because of her dramatics. Jenna thought carefully. Would she have ignored these dramatics? No, of course not. She would have phoned her straight away and reassured her. Right, she thought, nodding to herself, that's exactly what I need to do now.

Jenna scrolled to her recent contacts and tapped Susan's name, listening to the international dial tone with bated breath. "Susan?" she said as the line connected.

"Hi."

"Hey, how are you? Sorry, no, I know how you are. You're not great. I've listened to your voice messages. Okay, so gorgeous, where do I start?" Jenna sighed. "I want to start by reassuring you that—"

"How about you start by explaining the tequila dripping from your tits at two a.m. this morning."

Jenna sat upright. "What?"

"You heard me."

"What tequila? What are you talking about?"

"Well I'm looking at a picture of you topless, sitting on a bar with what looks like the barmaid pouring tequila down your chest and I think it looks like two women on their knees with their mouths open trying to catch the drips from your nipples."

"Susan! What are you talking about? What are you looking at?"

"Oh, and here's another one. Your bra's back on but it looks like you're leading some sort of conga with a huge inflatable penis between your legs. Oh, and here's another one of you in the background at the bar with a mystery blonde. And here you are again with two pint glasses wearing someone's sombrero."

Jenna could hear Susan tapping what she assumed was her laptop. "Susan. Stop. What are you looking at?"

"I don't know, Jenna. Why don't you tell me?"

Jenna rubbed her temples in the silence. "Has someone sent you some photos? Who would do that? Who would send you photos?"

"No, it's worse than that, Jenna. There are photos littering the internet of you practically naked for everyone to see."

"Where? On the Club Ski site? On the nightclub photo page? Where have you found these, Susan?"

"So you're not denying it then?"

"Susan, stop. Can we just calm down for a minute?"

"No we cannot calm down, Jenna! You're meant to be my girlfriend. You're meant to stay faithful."

"I have stayed faithful!"

"Have you?"

"Yes, Susan, I have!"

"I don't believe you."

"What?" Jenna shook her head, unable to follow what was going on.

"I said I don't believe you."

Jenna sighed. "You didn't believe me at ten forty-five last night, or ten forty-nine, or ten fifty-one, or—"

"So it's my fault then? You heard my stupid messages and just thought sod it?"

"No! I haven't done anything wrong!"

"What, apart from get naked and chat up blondes at the bar?"

"Susan, where have you seen these pictures?"

"They're available for everyone to see on Facebook."

"You're not on Facebook."

"I am now."

"You're snooping?"

"No, I'm making friends."

"With who?"

"Ouch," said Susan. "Was that a dig?"

"No! I meant which friends have shown you these pictures?"

"I found them."

"Where?"

"On Amber's site."

"You're friends with Amber? You're not friends with Amber, surely? You *must* have been snooping?"

"No. She has an open profile. Everyone can see everything she posts."

Jenna shook her head. "Only if you click on her site to snoop. Susan, I was calling to talk about your messages. They worried me."

"Really? Well this worries me."

"Why are you snapping? What have I done wrong?"

"You didn't call me! And now I know why!"

"I didn't take my phone out! I didn't know you'd left ten billion messages for me. I didn't get in until five a.m."

"Ten billion? So why couldn't you call, or text? Did you have company?"

"No! Susan stop! Just stop!"

"Fine. I'll stop," said Susan, ending the call.

****

Susan held the phone as tightly as she could. Her hand was shaking. Jenna had called too soon. Jenna had caught her off guard. She shook her head. Jenna hadn't denied it. She looked up at her laptop screen. How could she deny it? The evidence was there for all to see. She scrolled through the pictures, jumping as her phone rang again. She jabbed the answer button and started to speak. "I'm glad you've called back because there are more. You're—" Susan stopped as Jenna's strong voice interrupted her. It was calm and controlled, yet very firm.

"Can you tell me please, exactly what it is you think that I've done?"

Susan was disappointed that her voice sounded so shrill in comparison. "What haven't you done, Jenna? Look, there's another one here of you on some man's shoulders."

"So?"

"So?! So you're my girlfriend."

"And what would you like me to do?"

"I'd like you to show me some respect." Susan scrunched up her face as she realised how ridiculous that sounded.

"No problem," said Jenna, "I'll order a hijab from Amazon. Or would you prefer it if I went for the full length black burka instead? I'll walk ten paces behind you as well if you want."

Susan couldn't help but smile. "Stop it."

"Or I could wear a hijab *and* a burka, and I could finish off the look with a black bin bag, which would work quite well actually as the whole ensemble has to be waterproof if I'm skiing in it. But I'll only ski behind you, and I'll try and make sure the snow doesn't make too much noise as I slide over it."

"Stop it," said Susan unable to hold back a laugh.

"I'll look great shooting down the slopes in a big black burka. The dress bit can't be too long though as it might get tangled in my skis. I wonder if Amazon do different colours? It would be nice to mix it up a bit."

Susan laughed. "Okay, point taken. I'm sorry. I knew I sounded stupid the moment I said it."

"So why say it at all? Why say the things you said to me on the phone last night?"

Susan could feel herself blushing. "Like what?"

"Oh, that you're a total loser and you feel like you're dying."

"I am though, aren't I? I'm handling this all wrong."

"Can we Skype? Can you just listen?"

Susan nodded. "I'd like that. I'm sorry."

"I'm sorry too. Give me five minutes to fire up my laptop."

"Of course," said Susan, closing down the Facebook page and opening up the Skype tab instead. "See you in a minute."

"I look forward to it."

"Me too."

****

Jenna jumped off the bed and grabbed her laptop from the holdall that she still hadn't properly unpacked. She flipped the lid and switched it on, quickly pulling some pieces of A4 paper from the bottom drawer of her cabinet and reaching for a large felt marker. She started to write, clicking her computer in the direction of Skype as she went.

****

Susan sat on her tall stool and stretched out her arms. The vision of Jenna skiing the slopes in a full length body burka made her smile once more. *I'm such an idiot*, she said to herself as she replayed the conversation over in her mind. *I'm* the one who was snappy. *I'm* the one who was out of control. *I'm* the one who should be apologising. Susan looked at the screen and noticed that Jenna had come online. She clicked on her name and waited for the beeping to connect. Susan almost lost her breath as Jenna's face smiled out at her. It was as if she had forgotten how beautiful she really was. "Jenna I'm so sorry—"

Jenna put her finger to her lips and held up the first piece of paper. "SUSAN," it said.

Susan gasped. Jenna's eyes were smiling over the top of the writing. Susan watched as Jenna lifted the next piece of A4.

"I LOVE YOU." The writing was large, filling the screen.

"YOU ARE MY WORLD."

Susan bit her bottom lip as Jenna continued to lift sign after sign.

"MY EVERYTHING."

Susan smiled at the sicky face that had been drawn on the next one. "I GOT DRUNK."

Jenna lifted another sheet. "I'M SORRY."

Susan started to speak. "It's fine, I—" but Jenna returned her finger to her lips.

"BUT I PROMISE YOU THIS…"

"I WAS FAITHFUL."

"I WILL ALWAYS BE FAITHFUL."

"I'VE FOUND YOU NOW."

"AND I'M NEVER LETTING YOU GO."

Susan swallowed a tear at the drawing of the two stick women who had their arms wrapped around each other.

Jenna spoke for the first time. "Okay, last one. Are you ready?"

Susan nodded.

"Me in a burka." Jenna lifted the sketch of a mountain and an angry black scribble. She smiled. "I wasn't unfaithful, Susan, and I didn't deliberately not call. I only listened to your messages twenty minutes ago. My phone died and I've been out all day, and yes I did get drunk, but I just had fun with my friends, like I always do. I was talking about you all night, Susan. You have to believe me."

"I do. I'm sorry. It's me who should be apologising." She smiled. "You can put that sign down now." Susan watched as Jenna sheepishly lowered the drawing. "You are *so* beautiful and I'm such a total idiot."

"You? No, it's me. I promise you I had every intention of getting home early." She smiled. "I wanted to continue our FaceTime fun. But then two of the ski reps randomly got engaged so we started to celebrate."

"Jenna, you don't have to explain."

"I want to explain. I love you, Susan, and yes, it'll take us both a while to adjust and get this right. But we can, I know we can. I tried to call you this morning but my phone died and I was off all day with a group of execs and—"

"It's fine."

"Do you forgive me?"

Susan shook her head. "There's nothing to forgive. I'm the one with the crazy behaviour. I just acted like a totally controlling, insecure horror of a girlfriend."

Jenna sucked gently on her bottom lip. "Do you, umm, do you want to talk about it?"

"What? My emotional breakdown? No, not really. I just missed you."

"But you're going to miss me every day, I hope, and you can't keep calling yourself a friendless loser who's on death's door just because I'm not around."

Susan grimaced. "It wasn't quite like that, was it?"

"It was."

"I'm sorry. I just wanted to feel like I had a life. But it turns out I don't. Marcus bloody Ramsbottom has more of a life than I do."

"Oh, you said yesterday that I had to remind you about Marcus and Daisy."

Susan took a deep breath. "Well, Marcus is being investigated for inappropriate behaviour."

"About time too."

"And they want me to write a report."

"Good. Give him hell."

"No, he's a colleague."

"Yes, a shit one. What about Daisy?"

Susan smiled. "It's not as simple as that with Marcus."

"Yes it is. So what about Daisy?"

"No it isn't. He thinks I'm going to write him a glowing character reference."

"Well you're not. Tell me about Daisy. Remember Daisy, the one Marcus showed his tiny tiddler to?"

"He didn't, it was an accident."

"Irrelevant. Anyway. What's Daisy's news? Has she snared her boyfriend yet?"

Susan smiled. "You tell me. She said you gave her a plan."

"No, I just ordered her a spot of make-up. It should be arriving tomorrow."

"Jenna, you shouldn't have done that."

"I wanted to. They're tight for cash remember. Daisy was telling me how all of the other Year Sevens have started to wear mascara and eyeliner, so I bought her a beginner's make-up set. It's got tons of things in it. You should have seen her little face when she watched me click *buy*."

"Jenna, the girls are only allowed to wear a dab of blusher and a dash of mascara, and that's only in Year Nine and upwards."

"Oh they all wear it, Susan. It'll be fine."

"I'm not sure."

"It will be." Jenna smiled. "Everything will be fine, and I'm not just talking about little Daisy Button here. We're going to get this down. We're going to make this work."

"I hope so."

Jenna moved closer to the screen. "Trust me, Susan."

Susan smiled. "You know what? I do."

CHAPTER TWELVE

Susan was standing in front of the chalkboard in room 3A. Four days had passed since her slight argument with Jenna, and things were certainly looking up. They had managed to get into a nice routine of early morning phone call, afternoon Skype session, and late night text chat. Susan smiled to herself. Jenna was often hung over and half asleep during their morning calls, relying on the extra couple of hours in bed while Susan started her classes for the day. The afternoon Skype sessions were always lovely, with both relaying important information about their days, and Jenna occasionally having to explain a photo that Susan had accidentally spotted on someone else's timeline. But it was the late night texts chats that were the funniest. Very random and very raunchy, with Jenna mostly two sheets to the wind, encouraging Susan to misbehave.

Susan wrote the question, "Who believes in ghosts?" on the board, before taking a seat and waiting for her class. She smiled again, knowing that Jenna would be smiling too. It was love, and neither could deny it.

Susan felt the flutter of butterflies wash over her as her phone beeped once more. It was 2.00 p.m. in the UK which meant Jenna must have stopped for an afternoon break, and from this latest picture message it looked like she was in a wooden mountaintop toilet cubicle of sorts. She was holding her ski jacket up and pulling the braces from her salopettes taut over her breasts. **Come flick my bits**, was the caption.

Susan typed quickly. **I can't see any bits. Show me something worth seeing, and hurry. Class due any second. PS: How can you make ski gear look so hot???** Susan switched the phone to silent and stood up, welcoming the first of her Year Sevens into the room. "Smile," she said, "you've only got two lessons left."

The little girl looked shocked. Madam Quinn was never usually so cheery. "Are we still on God?" she asked.

Susan Quinn pointed at the board. "Sort of. We're looking more generally at beliefs today."

Margaret Beauchamp entered the room. "We're not still on God are we?"

"Is it more God stuff this week?" asked Prudence Frinton-Smith as she found her desk at the front.

"Girls, this is politics and philosophy. God's bound to crop up every now and then."

"It's God again," said Prudence Frinton-Smith to Cordelia Buckingham as Cordelia Buckingham took a seat next to her.

"Oh no," moaned two more girls, hearing the conversation as they entered the room.

Susan counted the heads. It was only Daisy Button missing. "We're approaching things differently this week." Susan thought back to her degree in Philosophy, Politics and Economics. The school had loved the fact she would be able to teach a broad range of subjects from religious education through to business studies. They had even made her take charge of some lower school Greek mythology and maths classes too. At least she had variety, she thought, pitying the teachers who took responsibility for one subject in its entirety. "So," she said, drawing on one of her philosophical arguments, "who believes in ghosts?"

"Perfect timing," said Margaret Beauchamp as Daisy Button hobbled into the room.

"What?" said Daisy.

"We're talking about ghosts," laughed Margaret.

Susan lifted her finger. "Enough. Daisy please take a seat."

Daisy adjusted herself on her crutches. "Am I okay to nip out again, Madam Quinn?" She whispered quietly. "I think I might need the toilet."

A couple of the girls sniggered.

"That's fine, Daisy." Susan waited for the little girl to leave the room before raising her voice. "You should be ashamed of yourselves. You, Margaret, for commenting, and you girls at the back, for laughing. Really. You're eleven and twelve, not two and three. I don't expect any silly playground behaviour now you're students at this school. Margaret I'll see you at the end."

The class stayed silent. "Right," said Susan, "where was I?" She pointed at the board. "Hands up if you believe in ghosts." Susan watched as every girl in the class lifted her hand. "And just remind me now. How many of you lifted your hand last week when I asked if you believed in God?" One solo hand at the back was raised. Susan nodded. "Okay then, why is it that you believe in ghosts, but you don't believe in God?"

Margaret Beauchamp waved her arm, eager to get back in the good books. "Because we have evidence of ghosts."

"Do we?"

Cordelia Buckingham nodded with authority. "My aunty has a poltergeist in her house."

"Really?" said Susan.

"Yes, she said that one night her cup of tea whizzed completely off the coffee table and spilt all over this new white rug that my uncle had just bought her."

Prudence Frinton-Smith rolled her eyes. "She probably just spilt it and didn't want to get into trouble."

"Did not."

Prudence Frinton-Smith upped the stakes. "Well my mum's friend, Sophina, said she saw a real ghost." She paused for the dramatics. "It was the ghost of her granny." She paused again. "Sitting in the back of her car." She took a deep breath. "When she was driving home, late one night." She lowered her voice for her final line. "From Tesco."

"Whatever," said Cordelia Buckingham, looking slightly shaken.

"Thank you, Prudence," said Susan, re-focusing the group. "But my question was, have any of *you* ever seen a ghost? For example, DAISY!" she gasped, as the little albino girl re-entered the room.

The whole class turned to look at the door.

"Daisy! What have you …" Susan paused, quickly deciding how best to handle the situation. "Why have you …"

None of the girls in the class dared laugh.

Susan settled for: "Are you okay?"

Daisy nodded and smiled, hobbling to her seat near the front of the room. "Fine thank you, Madam Quinn."

Susan struggled to tear her eyes away from Daisy's dark brown face. She looked like a poorly made up minstrel. "So," she said, trying to focus back on the question, "have any of you ever seen a ghost?" No one put their hand up, and Susan noticed Daisy sitting higher and prouder in her seat. "Right," she said, still stealing glances at the streaky jawline and neck, "you've never seen a ghost, yet you still believe they exist, based on other people's reports?" A couple of the girls nodded. "So what about all of the people who say they've seen God? All of the people who believe they've had near death experiences? All the people who cite God as the reason for their child's miraculous recovery, or the reason for them having cheated death, like the voice in the darkness that stopped them from walking off the edge of a cliff?"

Daisy put up her hand. "Because people find the impossible easier to believe than the improbable."

Susan was shocked. Daisy was usually so quiet in class. Her new found tan was obviously giving her confidence. "Can you explain that?"

Daisy nodded and turned in her seat to better address her classmates. "My Grandma told me this once."

Susan could see the girls at the back trying desperately hard not to laugh. They had that look of panic on their faces with flared nostrils and sucked in bottom lips, betraying the shaking in their stomachs and the choking in their throats.

Daisy swept her fine white fringe from her brow and began. "Imagine a huge Boeing 747 aeroplane in perfect working order. Imagine it lands in a field and gets taken apart piece by piece, screw by screw. Imagine all the pieces are laid out on the grass."

Susan looked at the girls. Daisy was holding their attention and it wasn't just because of the mask of heavy-duty midnight-brown foundation she'd rubbed all over her face. "Okay," said Susan encouraging her to continue.

"So, what are the chances of a whirlwind or tornado passing through that field and whipping that plane back together into perfect working order?" Daisy waited for someone to answer.

Margaret Beauchamp lifted her hand. "Zero. As if a tornado could screw in the screws or put all of the seats and toilets back in the right place."

"Or put those little leaflets behind the seats," added Prudence. "You know, the ones with the menus on, and the ones with the safety stuff on."

"It's impossible," said Daisy, nodding and turning back to the front.

Susan frowned. "You said people are more likely to believe the impossible than the improbable."

Daisy shrugged. "I know. What's more difficult to make? A Boeing 747 aeroplane, or the whole of our planet with all of its perfectly designed eco systems that let us live our lives?"

"Daisy!" Susan was in shock. "I think you're touching on the teleological argument for the existence of God."

"No, I'm just saying that if you don't think a plane can be whipped up by a whirlwind even when all of the pieces are laid out and ready to go, then how can you think the whole world just appeared out of nowhere with a big bang in space? It's impossible, but people would rather believe that than the improbable."

"And what's the improbable?"

Daisy shrugged. "The little old man, with a beard, on a cloud."

Susan sat down on her desk. "Has anyone got anything they'd like to add to that splendid, splendid, analogy?"

Margaret Beauchamp lifted her hand. "Can I have some of what she's having?"

"It's called Espresso Chocolate foundation," whispered Daisy, reaching into her bag, "by Maybelline."

CHAPTER THIRTEEN

Susan waited for the Year Seven class to leave before addressing the two girls still sitting at the front. "Margaret, could I have a word outside, please? Daisy, I'll be back in a moment."

Margaret Beauchamp slid from her chair and kept her head bowed as she left the room. "I'm sorry, Madam Quinn," she said from the safety of the corridor, "I know I shouldn't have called Daisy a ghost."

"It's meanness, Margaret, and meanness is a horrible trait to have."

"I'm not mean, Madam Quinn. I was just trying to be funny."

"At someone else's expense. A joke's only a joke if everyone's playing along."

Margaret kept her head low. "I know. I've learnt my lesson. I didn't say anything about her make-up when she came back in, did I?"

"No, you didn't, so thank you for that. I'll be having a word with Daisy and I'd like you to promise me you won't tease her again. Ever."

"I won't, Madam Quinn." Margaret lifted her eyes. "She really impressed me in there."

"Yes, me too. Now hurry along to your next lesson. You're incredibly lucky you didn't get a detention."

Margaret's face turned as white as Daisy's pre-foundation natural look. "Thank you, Madam Quinn. I'd hate to get a detention. I've never had a detention before, and my dad—"

"Daisy's going to be a couple of minutes late. Let your teacher know please."

"Yes, Madam Quinn, I really am sorry."

"Just be kind to her, Margaret."

"I will, Madam Quinn. I'm so, so sorry."

"Find a way of showing Daisy you're sorry, not me."

Margaret was almost curtseying with each apologetic nod. "I will, Madam Quinn. I will."

Susan watched as the Year Seven girl trotted quickly down the corridor. She tutted to herself and turned back around, glancing momentarily through the glass panel in the door. She looked again, wondering where Daisy Button might have gone, before realising the little girl was actually camouflaged between the mahogany bookcase and the brown *layers of life* soil poster.

"I'm going to be late for my lesson," said Daisy as Susan re-entered the room.

"Don't worry. I've passed along a message." Susan paused. "Daisy, you know make-up's not allowed in school, don't you?"

The whites of Daisy's eyes grew larger. "What make-up?"

"The Maybelline Espresso Chocolate foundation you were so proudly showing Margaret just then."

"Jenna bought it for me and I love it." She nodded quickly. "Didn't you see the way the girls were listening to me? I never usually hold anyone's attention unless they're staring at my white skin."

Susan sat down next to the little girl. "Daisy, they were listening to you because you were making some really good points. Your argument was really clever."

"I don't usually have the confidence to talk much in class." Daisy swooshed her pale fringe from her forehead and smiled proudly. "But now I do."

"Daisy, I'm going to have to ask you to wipe it off."

"I can't. Please, Madam Quinn. For the very first time I feel good about myself."

"Oh, Daisy, listen, make-up's against school rules. I'm not being deliberately mean." Susan stood up and walked towards her desk, opening the bottom drawer and pulling out a packet of wet wipes. "You're going to have to take it off."

Daisy tipped her school bag upside down. "It's not like I'm wearing any of *this* stuff."

Susan watched as a mountain of glitters, powders, nail polishes and eye shadows dropped onto the table. "That's all from Jenna?"

"It came in a pack. It's called Maybelline's Midnight Glitter Glam."

"Daisy, it's not midnight, and glitter's not really that glam." Susan smiled at the little girl. "You're eleven. You're at that age where you want to experiment with different looks—"

"I haven't got time to experiment. I'm seeing Timmy tomorrow. We're helping Bob with the bushes, and last week Timmy was talking about a skate park he goes to on a Sunday afternoon, and I really want him to invite me."

"Daisy, you've got to do this in your own time."

"I can't. My mum won't let me wear make-up. She says my skin's too sensitive."

Susan frowned. "How sensitive?"

"I have to use all of these special soaps and creams, and sometimes if I've been cuddling my Grandma's cheeks too much I get a rash."

"Daisy, we need to get this off." Susan quickly pulled a wipe out of the packet.

Daisy squinted at the pink writing. "No. I can't use these. They're not hypoallergenic."

"Well I doubt the Espresso Chocolate foundation is either. Come on," said Susan, sweeping all of the make-up back into the little girl's school bag. "Let's get you to the bathroom."

Daisy pulled herself up and hobbled after her teacher, desperately trying to ignore the burning sensation and strange twitch around her cheeks.

****

Jenna pulled to a sharp hockey stop at the bottom of the Chavannes Express. "You guys go ahead." She spoke to the three male execs. "I'll wait for Jade."

"Is it a long lift?" asked Bill, the oldest of the group, as he lined himself up against the metal barriers.

"It's the longest in the area," shouted Jenna, watching the men shuffling forwards as the barrier dropped. "That's why I'm waiting for Jade. You lot drank my hipflask dry yesterday."

"We'll have a swig at the top then," came the shout, as the chairlift swept around the corner and scooped the three skiers up and away.

Jenna turned back around and scanned the slope for the petite blonde. It didn't look like she was over the ridge yet, so she pulled off a glove and reached into her jacket pocket for her phone instead. She tapped the screen. Susan still hadn't replied to the second picture message she'd sent. This time she'd pulled her jacket, ski vest AND sport bra up, yanked her salopette braces into the middle of her chest, and pressed a finger onto an erect nipple. She'd added the caption: **Fine, I'll flick my own bits then.** Jenna glanced up at the slope before typing another message: **Tell me what you want to see next. I'll show you ANYTHING.**

Jenna dropped the phone back into her pocket and scanned the slope once more, spotting the pink hat first and the trademark wide turns second. She smiled and pulled her glove back on. The lady banker hadn't been drawn into any form of competition with her male counterparts, no matter the extent of their teasing. They had compared her to the lady from the Ski yoghurt advert, gracefully carving her way down the slopes with her long blonde hair fluttering in the breeze, when all they really wanted to see was her with knees bent, bottom out, haring down the hill all hell for leather. Jade hadn't risen to their ribbing though and continued to ski at her own pace in the same calm and controlled manner she was revered for at work.

"Hey, we're heading up the Chavannes now," said Jenna as Jade slowed to a stop next to her.

"Have they gone ahead?"

Jenna nodded and sidestepped across the snow towards the metal barriers. "It's the longest lift in the area and I didn't want a repeat of yesterday's 'who can gulp the most brandy' competition."

Jade pulled her tinted ski goggles up onto her hat. "It's okay, I'm a sipper." She caught Jenna's eyes. "I like to take my time."

"I've noticed," said Jenna with a grin, pushing herself through the barrier.

"Hey, don't you tease me too!"

Jenna pulled herself forwards with her poles and slid towards the red line, checking her position as she waited for the next chairlift to swing around the corner. "It's all part of the job description."

Jade stepped into the lane next to Jenna. "And what else is in the job description? You don't mind if I sit next to you, do you?"

"No," said Jenna as the six-seater chairlift hit the back of their thighs, scooping them up into the air. "Heads up, I'm pulling the safety bar down."

Jade leaned backwards. "Anything else you'd like to pull down?"

"Umm," Jenna laughed. "You're actually the first female banker I've met. I thought you lot were meant to be stuffy."

Jade pulled off a glove and reached into her top pocket, taking out a small white business card. "We're heading into Morzine tonight. I'd love it if you'd join us for a drink. I'm utterly fed up with the company of men." She handed it to Jenna.

Jenna studied the print on the card. **Jade Wharton. Investment Banker.** There were three different phone numbers and an email address all printed neatly underneath a gold diamond that had a gold letter S inside. "I thought you guys didn't have your mobiles with you?"

Jade reached over Jenna's lap and tilted the card. "I've written the phone number for my hotel room on the back."

Jenna looked down at the dainty fingers and pretty pink nails that were hovering between her legs. "I think we're heading out to Les Gets tonight."

"Tomorrow then," said Jade, twisting her body even more towards Jenna's.

"Okay," said Jenna, "might work." She pushed the card into her jacket pocket and took out her hip flask. "Drink?"

"Always." Jade smiled seductively and took the offering, slowly twisting the lid between her first finger and thumb.

Jenna watched the deliberately sexy action, trying desperately hard not to imagine her nipple in place of the lid. "Have you enjoyed your trip so far?" she asked instead.

Jade lifted the flask to her mouth and gently let her tongue dart out to catch the first drip. She sipped slowly and licked her lips. "You've been wonderful. Your knowledge of the area's incredible. You've been insightful, and witty." She paused. "And the way you've handled those men has taught *me* a lesson or two. It's very difficult for feminine lesbians like us to get the balance right. We don't want to encourage their advances, yet we don't want the label of man hating feminist." She smiled. "You play the buddy card, Jenna. You're great at diffusing their misplaced innuendos with humour and—"

"Sorry, you're a lesbian?"

"Yes, aren't you?"

Jenna coughed. "Well, yes, but I was asking if you'd enjoyed the scenery and the snow conditions, and the après ski—"

"Jenna, you've been the highlight of this trip for me. I've never met someone who's as sporty, yet sexy, as you are. You've got this natural beauty that draws the eye and your features are so striking that you honestly don't need an ounce of makeup." She paused and angled her body even closer. "I bet you look utterly sensational on a night out though."

Jenna shuffled in her seat, heavily restricted by the metal bar that was pinning her into position. She glanced down at the rows of tall pines wondering how best to diffuse *this* situation. "Hey, have you heard the joke about the tree?" She paused. "It's sappy."

Jade smiled. "I'm not a man. I'm not easily distracted."

"The clouds?"

"You're going to sit here and tell me a joke about the clouds?"

Jenna nodded. "Yes. Where do clouds go to the bathroom?"

Jade tried not to smile. "I don't know. Where do clouds go to the bathroom?"

"Anywhere they want."

"Poor."

"The mountain?"

"No, stop. I don't want to hear about the mountain."

Jenna smiled. "Yes you do. What did the little mountain say to the big mountain?"

"Hi Cliff?"

"Yes!" laughed Jenna.

Jade rolled her eyes. "You've got enough to get us all the way to the top, haven't you?"

Jenna nodded. "Sure have."

"She's a lucky lady."

"Who?"

"Whoever it is you're shunning me for."

"I'm not shunning you, but yes, she's called Susan, and she's very special indeed."

"And she likes your shit jokes, does she?"

Jenna smiled. "I haven't told you my shit joke."

"I don't want to hear it."

"Yes you do."

Jade laughed. "Oh no, this gets worse. You're funny as well. Sporty, sexy, fit, and funny. Life's so cruel to me."

"Hey, I haven't even said it yet."

"Fine, tell me your shit joke."

Jenna coughed and prepared herself. "I'm one of those people who likes to read while taking a shit." She smiled widely. "That's the reason I'm banned from Waterstones."

Jade banged her on the arm and swallowed her laughter. "That's gross."

"It helps though, hey. Look," she said, nodding at the mound of snow up ahead, "we're nearly at the top."

"Is it a long term thing? You and this Susan woman?"

"It will be," said Jenna, with meaning.

****

Susan dropped another brown-stained paper towel into the sink. She crouched down and looked at Daisy's face, trying her best not to grimace. "Oh, Daisy, you're ever so sore. I don't want to rub too hard, but I think I might need one more go at these streaks."

The little girl's short white eyelashes were blinking quickly. "When can I put my glasses back on? I'm totally blind without them."

"Let me have one more go," said Susan, running more warm water. She crouched back down and started to dab.

"Ouch," said Daisy flinching with the pain.

"I'm really sorry," said Susan, "but I think we should go to the school nurse." She passed over Daisy's glasses and reached into the sink to squeeze out the paper towels. She dropped them in the bin in the corner and swilled the sink with her fingers.

Daisy Button was open mouthed in front of the mirror. "I look like a ladybird."

Susan glanced at Daisy's reflection, unable to ignore the way her round spectacles stood out from her bright red face. "You don't."

"I do. I look like a ladybird that's landed in a muddy puddle. Timmy won't fancy me now."

"Timmy's a gardener. He likes nature." Susan heard how ridiculous she sounded. "Ignore that. Nurse Watts will sort you out. Come on, Daisy." She put her arm around the little girl's shoulder and helped her out of the toilets. "It's not as bad as you think."

"WHAT in the name of St Wilfred's has happened to you?!" Vice Principal Dorothy Brown screeched to a halt in the corridor. "Do we have an orang-utan on the loose?"

"Daisy's had an allergic reaction. I'm popping her down to Nurse Watts."

"You're not teaching?"

"No, I've finished for the day."

"So the report's done I take it."

Susan frowned. "Report?"

"Yes. The report on Professor Ramsbottom's ski trip conduct, or dare I say, lack of it. I need it on my desk by six p.m. at the very latest." Vice Principal Brown peered down at the little girl. "Close your ears, young lady."

"Today?"

"Yes, today! Investigations don't run themselves, Madam Quinn. I need facts. I need evidence. I need intricate details of every misdemeanour and every wrongdoing. I need examples!" The broad-shouldered old battle-axe shook her jowls. "I need details of Professor Ramsbottom's inappropriate behaviour and I need them now!"

"It wasn't his fault," said Daisy with wide eyes.

Dorothy Brown glowered. "What wasn't? When?"

"When I walked into his room. When I saw him naked."

CHAPTER FOURTEEN

Susan checked the star-shaped clock hanging from the wall in her school apartment. It was 4.50 p.m. Jenna would be Skyping in ten minutes. She linked her fingers together and stretched out her arms, looking at her laptop screen at the report she'd been struggling with for the past hour. Vice Principal Dorothy Brown had almost blown a gasket when she'd heard little Daisy Button's comment, pulling the girl straight into her office and making her dictate an exact account of what had happened that night on the ski trip. Susan had stayed seated at the side of the room, unsure if it was Daisy's cheeks or her own that were emitting the most heat. It had sounded so dreadful. Daisy had seen her teacher naked. She had seen Professor Ramsbottom with no clothes on, because Professor Ramsbottom thought it was Madam Quinn entering the room. Professor Ramsbottom thought it was Madam Quinn who was knocking. Only it wasn't Madam Quinn, it was little Daisy Button instead.

It had sounded so seedy. The idea that Madam Quinn and Professor Ramsbottom might have been having some extra-curricular fun of their own, as Vice Principal Brown had so delicately phrased it. Susan had been quick to correct her assumption, which then caused another huge onslaught about how he was therefore a sexual predator and must be suspended for sexual harassment, especially since Susan was now of the homosexual variety. Dorothy Brown had been beaming with glee, completely oblivious to both Susan and Daisy's pain, declaring it yet another nail in 'that little man's' coffin, and insisting Susan's report be factual yet full.

Susan re-read her three key headings. The first said: **Professor Ramsbottom's conduct with staff.** The second said: **Professor Ramsbottom's conduct with students.** The third said: **Additional examples of inappropriate professional conduct.** Dorothy Brown had been very clear about the layout of the report, and Susan had tried her best to write three detailed paragraphs under the headings she'd been given, but it was hard. It was hard to be factual without sounding like she was putting the boot in completely. She read it again, cringing at her own comments. Was there really any need to disclose the fact that Marcus had tried to tweezer her nipples as he held her horizontally for the group photo at the French service station? Was there really any need to discuss Marcus's continued pursual of a one-sided relationship with her? Susan sighed and pressed delete. Marcus wasn't a sexual predator. Yes, he might have compared Willamena Edgington to Pamela Anderson in the game of ski pass recognition, and he did make that one private comment comparing Eugenie Roehampton's body to that of Dolly Parton's, but these weren't evidence of a sexual predator, just signs of a slightly misguided, typical bloke. Susan sighed again. Was that typical bloke behaviour? She didn't really know. Her experience with the male species was probably as limited as his was with the female species. It was so hard. She had to write the facts, but maybe she'd just write the facts that were public. Marcus's ski pants split in front of the group and they all caught sight of his bottom. Susan nodded. Fact. Marcus called Daisy Button into his room and she caught sight of him naked. Fact. But he didn't know it was her entering the room. Fact.

Susan jumped as the Skype app suddenly filled her screen. Jenna's jpeg was smiling at her. She connected the call and leaned backwards in her chair. "Hey, beautiful," she said as she waved at the screen.

"Hey, gorgeous," said Jenna, returning the customary greeting they always slipped in to. "What a day I've had! I've got so much to tell you. Remember that lady in my group? Jade? The banker? Well she gave me her number today, and I'd like you to know I dropped it in the very first bin I saw!" Jenna was beaming proudly. "Are you okay, gorgeous? I didn't flirt back. She was actually being really cheesy with me and the whole thing made me cringe. I ended up telling her a load of really crap jokes just to pass the time on the chairlift."

Susan smiled. "I'm fine. I believe you. Thanks for telling me."

"Hey, you said you'd rather know everything."

"No honestly, it's fine. I've just had a bit of a tough day, that's all."

"Oh gorgeous, tell me everything." Jenna's face became bigger in the screen. "Is that why you haven't replied to my picture messages?"

Susan smiled. "Sorry, yes, they're incredible, and yes, I do want some more. It's just been non-stop since this afternoon what with Daisy's allergic reaction to your make-up—"

"What?"

"She dolled herself up with some chocolate brown foundation and waltzed into my lesson like Beyoncé Knowles." Susan paused. "Actually she hobbled in, but still. She was swishing her fringe and all sorts. Bless her, she thought she looked great."

"And did she?"

"Jenna! She's an albino. You bought her Espresso Chocolate foundation."

"It was part of a pack. I didn't know what was in it."

"Anyway, she's fine. Danielle Watts sorted her out with some cooling cream."

Jenna tried not to laugh. "So, what else happened today?"

"Oh just this report about Marcus. Dorothy Brown caught me in the corridor. Daisy overheard the conversation and thought Dorothy was talking about her."

"In what way?"

"Oh I don't know. Dorothy was going on about his inappropriate behaviour." Susan paused. "I mean, you can't really get more inappropriate than calling someone into your room whilst you're sitting there spread eagle with nothing but a sneering grin on your face."

"So wrong."

"Dorothy told me I had until six to get the report on her desk. Daisy must have assumed it had something to do with her." Susan rolled her eyes. "But Daisy even said that Marcus was waiting for me."

"Naked?"

"Exactly! I had to convince Dorothy that we were not, and never have been, an item, which now means she's pressuring me to do him for sexual harassment."

"And so you should!"

"Jenna, he's harmless."

"He's not!"

"He is. He's just a bit inappropriate at times."

Jenna was frowning. "And that's okay is it?"

"Well it's not grounds for him to lose his job."

"Who's made the actual formal complaint against him?"

Susan shook her head. "I don't know, and Dorothy had no idea about the Daisy Button incident, so it wasn't her or her mum. But thankfully she approved of how I'd handled the situation, so thank you again for that. You were the one who made me call Mrs Button, remember?"

Jenna shuddered. "Can we stop talking about him now?"

"Suits me," said Susan with a smile. "Remind me what this Jade woman of yours looks like again."

Jenna grinned. "Blonde, slim, really pretty blue eyes, pink lips."

"And you ditched her number?"

"Of course I did. I've got my very own slim, pert-titted, hazel-nutty-brown-haired-beauty of my own right here."

"You've got such a way with words."

"S-s-sorry, y-y-your breaking u-up." The image of Jenna was flashing on the screen. "S-s-say t-t-that again?"

Susan leaned in closer and spoke louder. "I said you've got a great way with words."

"W-w-what?"

Susan checked her computer's connection. Five bars. "It must be you, beautiful. I've got good signal."

Jenna had become pixelated. "L-l-let me c-c-call you b-b-back."

Susan watched as the blurred image disappeared from the screen. She jumped down from her stool and dashed to the fridge, grabbing a can of Diet Coke and making it back to the counter just in time to connect the call.

"A-a-any b-b-better?" Jenna was still made up of boxes and the image on the screen was flashing.

Susan went to reply when the connection cut out once more. She typed a message into the Skype conversation box instead: "Shall I try you?"

Jenna typed back: **Yes.**

Susan clicked on the video call button, opening her can and taking a sip of drink as she waited. The tone kept bleeping but the connection never came. She ended the call and typed instead: "Shall I call your mobile?"

It's dead. All those picture messages I sent you. Let me put it on charge.

"So," typed Susan, continuing to use the Skype's messaging service, "you were telling me about my pert-titted beautiness."

I meant every word. You're stunning, Susan.

"You are. You make ski gear look so sexy."

I'm sexier out of it.

"I know you are."

You want to see?

"Always." Susan smiled as she took another sip of drink. "OMG," she typed, slamming the can back down on the counter and absorbing the full impact of the shot that had just appeared on her screen. "You are SO hot, Jenna!"

You want to see more?

Susan leaned closer into the laptop screen, unable to draw her eyes away from the naked breasts. "Can anyone see this?" she typed.

No. This is our private Skype conversation. Stop worrying.

"You're so hot. Seriously, how are you my girlfriend?"

Because you're stunning too.

"I'm not."

You are. You're sexy. You're smart. You're AMAZING in bed.

"You're making me blush over here."

Good, let's see if I can make you blush some more.

"Okay," typed Susan, "give me your best." She felt her heart quicken, fully aware that Jenna would be getting herself into some crazy position and snapping away with her webcam. Susan smiled to herself and clicked on her laptop's own camera button, leaning back in shock as her face filled the screen. What was Jenna thinking? She wasn't sexy. In fact her hair looked flatter than usual and any remnants of this morning's make-up had well and truly rubbed off. She twisted herself sideways on her stool and flicked her head down between her legs, coming back up and checking the result on the screen. *Shit*, she thought, *I look like a scarecrow.* "Damn it," she said, trying to comb it through with her fingers. Susan heard the Skype message ping and minimised her webcam.

How's this for starters?

Susan gasped. Jenna must have moved her laptop onto her dressing table as the shot filling her screen was of Jenna lying naked on the bed. "How did you take that?" she typed.

Three second time delay on the webcam. Yours will have it too ;) ;) ;)

"I don't even take good face shots."

Show me something else then.

Susan smiled and clicked back on the camera. She tilted the laptop screen down slightly and opened the top three buttons of her shirt. She pressed the snap shot button and smiled at the image, pleased that she was wearing a push up bra. She clicked back on Skype and typed: "How's this?" before adding the first picture from her webcam's photo roll.

!!!!!!! YOU ARE THE SEXIEST LADY I KNOW SUSAN QUINN !!!!!!!!

Susan blushed. "Am not."

You SO are. Do you have ANY idea what you do to me?

"Tell me."

You turn me on.

Susan jumped off the stool and knelt over the sofa, quickly drawing together her curtains before checking the lock on her door. She clicked back on the webcam tab and sat back down, lowering the laptop screen even further. She undid the rest of her buttons and drew her shirt out to the sides. She took another shot and added it to her next message. "Wish you were here."

SERIOUSLY Susan, you are INCREDIBLE! I'd pull you so close into me if I was there. Your stomach looks amazing, your boobs look amazing, you're just amazing!

Susan pulled off her shirt and unclipped her bra, drawing one foot underneath her into a slight kneeling position on the stool. She pushed herself upwards and stuck out her chest, clicking on the snapshot button and looking at the result. She frowned. Her right boob looked droopy because she was leaning in to take the shot. She clicked on the three second timer button instead and moved her hands behind her head, arching her back and pushing her boobs forward. The picture took and she looked at the screen, pleasantly surprised by the result. Susan dropped back onto her bottom and started to type. "You couldn't see my boobs in that last picture."

Okay then, they look amazing in your bra.

"Do you WANT to see my boobs?"

WHAT?????

"Do you?"

OMG ALWAYS

"You're sure this is safe?"

I've just sent a picture of me lying naked on the bed. It's safe.

Susan smiled to herself. "You turn me on too," she typed before adding her photo to the message.

SERIOUSLY SUSAN!!!! I NEED TO CALL YOU!!!

"Let me build you into more of a sweat first."

Really????

"Yes, really." Susan moved herself back into the position on her knee, this time undoing the top button of her trousers and pulling down on the zip. She pressed the three second countdown button before grabbing a nipple with one hand and thrusting the other down the front of her pants. She gasped at herself as she saw the image on the screen. "Want you," she typed, as she added the picture to the message.

WOW WOW WOW WOW WOW WOW WOW. I want to show you how turned on you're making me.

Susan smiled and typed "Okay," before jumping off the stool and grabbing the throw from her bed. She wrapped it around her shoulders and waited with a nervous shiver, feeling the electricity sear across her chest as she heard the ping of her Skype. She leaned into the screen with an open mouth. Jenna was bent over, touching her toes, and there was a clear glistening visible between her legs. Susan released the throw and started to type. "Need you, like that, right now."

Jenna's reply was almost immediate: **Touching myself for you.**

Susan pulled off her trousers and pants, and used the stool to climb onto the counter. She tilted the screen as far back as it would go and knelt down, straddling the laptop. She pressed the countdown button and held her breath. The picture took and she twisted herself back around, sitting down on the counter. She cringed slightly at the image on the screen, but decided to send it all the same. "Sorry, it looks like a slab of meat. Pork chop maybe." She shivered and rubbed her legs, tingling for a different reason when her Skype pinged again. She read the message.

Fingers inside me.

Susan felt her stomach lunge at the image Jenna had attached.

"Sorry, I'll be sexier," she typed, realising her last pork chop picture could simply not compete. "Give me a minute." She stood back up on the counter and straddled the screen, this time standing up tall, almost hitting her head on her Moroccan pendant lamp as she pressed the countdown button. She kept one hand on her hip and moved the other hand behind her and down past her bottom. She bent her fingers and pushed them between her legs from the back. The picture took but she shrieked out as a loud bang sounded behind her. Susan wobbled on the counter and grabbed her bare breasts, staring at the door handle, half expecting it to fly open and whoever was there to catch her in the strangest position. She glanced up. Maybe she could say she was changing the bulb.

"Can I come in?"

Susan squealed in a complete panic. "Give me a second."

"It's me."

Susan watched in horror as the handle started to move. The door shook and the voice was back.

"It's locked. Come on, Susan, this is important."

Susan scrambled off the counter and grabbed her clothes, throwing them on as quickly as she could. "Coming," she shouted, as she straightened her hair and fastened her final few buttons. She reached for the throw and slung it onto the counter, instantly hiding her laptop. Susan glanced around the room to check for any stray underwear, or other evidence of her actions, before unlocking the door. She deliberately stood with her foot outstretched so it would only open an inch. "How can I help?"

Marcus Ramsbottom pushed his way into her kitchen. "Why are your curtains closed?"

"This is my apartment. I can close my curtains whenever I like."

Marcus sniffed and glanced around the room. "Where's best to sit? I always feel like I'm in one of those incense shops when I come in here."

"What can I help you with, Marcus?" Susan was still standing at the door.

Marcus bent down and opened her fridge. "You don't mind if I have one of these do you?" he asked, already twisting the screw cap on the bottle of Bud.

Susan gave up and shut the door. She glanced at the sofa, then the bed, before pointing to the tall stools next to the counter. "Sit down. What can I help you with?"

Marcus let out a tut. "Bloody Battle-Axe Brown hauled me in for another meeting."

"And?" said Susan, sitting down next to him.

"A parent's complained about me, and now it seems like she's trying to dredge up all sorts." He took a quick sip of the beer. "She's losing it I tell you. She's like that old man from Shawshank Redemption who can't stand the thought of leaving the prison because he's so institutionalised."

"Getting you fired won't mean she stays. She's retiring. She'll be gone by the summer."

Marcus scrunched up his face. "Who said anything about getting me fired? She's just trying to have her last power trip before she goes. Trying to make up for that time I rejected her."

"Oh, Marcus, don't be so ridiculous." Susan paused as she watched his moustache twitching. He was nervous. "Who's complained?"

Marcus took another quick sip of beer. "Willamena Edgington's parents."

"Really? What was their complaint?"

"Her parents check her Facebook account. We're friends on there. They didn't think it was *appropriate* so they contacted the school."

"You're friends on Facebook? With Willamena Edgington? From Year Eleven?"

"She added me."

"You didn't have to accept her."

"Oh, Susan, it's not a big deal. Lots of teachers make friends with their students on social media. I like to be accessible to those I'm educating in a variety of different ways."

Susan coughed and walked towards the counter. "Have you been, umm, have you been interacting?"

"No! Not like that!"

"So delete her. If you've done nothing wrong then you've got nothing to worry about."

Marcus pulled on his ginger moustache. "Exactly, exactly. Twitter's so much more popular with the young people nowadays anyway. But I think it's best if I start to gather a few character statements from people who know me. From people who've worked with me. From people I trust to give an accurate account of my character." Marcus pricked up his ears. "What's that pinging noise?" He nodded. "There it is again." He glanced under the counter, then back up, scanning the work surface. "Do you have a phone under here?" he said, moving the throw to the floor.

"No, it's my …" Susan tried to reach out and grab the laptop, but it was too late, Marcus was pulling up the screen.

"What in heaven's name is that?" he said, tilting his head at the image.

Susan tried to grab it again but he was holding it open. "Marcus, let go please."

"Is it a pork chop?" He frowned. "No wait, what are those? Fingers? Oh goodness, is that …"

Susan managed to minimise the webcam, gasping loudly as her Skype filled the screen. Jenna had sent through a string of photos with the captions: **Two fingers. Three Fingers. Coming for you.**

"Marcus!" she shouted, grappling with him for control.

"My oh my, what sites have you been accessing?"

"It's my personal Skype, now let go!"

"Mon amie, hang on un momento," Marcus was leaning in closer to the images and flaring his nostrils. "So, your Skype name's Susan dot Quinn. I'll make sure I add you."

"Marcus!" she shouted, somehow managing to minimise the Skype screen as well.

"Susan?" Marcus frowned. "Susan, what's this?" He leaned backwards and took in the three main headings on the Word document. "A report into my behaviour?" He glanced sideways. "You're writing a report into my professional conduct on the ski trip?" He continued to read, gasping in shock at the text. "Susan!" he shouted. "How dare you!"

CHAPTER FIFTEEN

Marcus let go of the laptop screen and shook his head. "Susan, you traitor."

Susan slammed the lid closed and pointed at the door. "Please leave."

"Why? So you can add to your document and twist that knife even deeper."

"No, because you've come in here and invaded my privacy." Susan was shaking. "Please leave."

"What possessed you to write those terrible things?"

"Marcus, they're facts. Trust me I could have written an awful lot more."

"Why?" Marcus was frantically running his fingers through his hair. "Why would you do this to me? We're colleagues. We're friends."

"Dorothy Brown gave me the headings. I'm sure she's asked the same of your head of department and your head of house. It's just form filling, Marcus."

"You could have said no."

"She knows about the Daisy Button incident. She wants me to confirm the facts. She needs—"

"You told her!" Marcus was now pulling on his moustache. "I thought it was you at the door!"

"That's what I've written, and no, I didn't tell her."

Marcus jumped down from the stool and started to pace. "This is unbelievable, Susan. I thought I could count on you. Crikey, what a fool. I came round here tonight to ask for a character statement. I thought you'd back me up, just like I've backed you up in the past." He paused and pointed his finger. "The services. You left Daisy Button behind. I'll tell them."

Susan twisted around. "What?"

"I'll tell them. I'll report you. You'll be disciplined, possibly fired." He was shaking his head and pacing quickly. "Now *that's* a real cause for investigation. Teacher leaves eleven year old student stranded at a foreign service station." He stood still and pointed his finger again. "Refuse to hand in the report, or I'll tell them."

Susan stepped towards the door. "Marcus, I'd like you to leave."

"I'll tell them, you know I will. You'll never work again!"

"YOU were the second in command. YOU were the one who cleared them out of the services. YOU were the one who said they were all present." Susan shook, angry at her own outburst.

"Ooo, look at you losing your cool. Sore point is it?" He bared his stubby yellow teeth in a sneering grin. "That's right, you were flustered by Jenna. The moment your lesbian affair started your professional responsibilities flew out the window."

"Marcus, you were just as much to blame. But it was Jenna and I who sorted it out. Daisy was fine. No one knew. No one knows. No one *has* to know."

"They won't know if you change that report."

Susan gasped. "I can't change it. They're the facts."

"Fine, well add some positives in there too. That's the least you can do for me."

"Like what? Like the way you barge into my room? The way you use physical force to view my private messages?"

"Good point, my mon amie. What if I tell them you're accessing pornographic sites via the school's Wi-Fi?"

"Marcus! I haven't been accessing pornographic sites! I'm talking on a private Skype message to my girlfriend, and it's none of your business."

"You're sending filthy pictures."

Susan was shaking. "I'm sending in the report and it'll be fact based. No more, no less."

"Add some positives or I'll tell them everything I know."

"No."

"What?"

"I said no." Susan turned to the counter, startled as her phone burst to life. She lifted it with shaking hands and answered the call, silencing its singing. "H-h-hey."

Jenna's voice sounded in her ear. "Hey, gorgeous, are you okay? You stopped messaging. Did I go too far?"

Susan watched as Marcus folded his arms. "I-I-I'm fine. Marcus is here."

"Marcus? Are you okay? I hope you put your clothes on before you answered the door."

"I-I-I'm fine."

"Susan?"

Marcus spoke loudly. "She'll be fine if she does the right thing."

"Susan? Did he just say something? What's going on?"

"I'm fine. Really."

Marcus spoke again. "Good choice, my mon amie."

Susan moved the phone away from her ear and covered the receiver. "I'm sending in the report."

"No, you're not," said Marcus.

Susan lifted the phone back to her mouth. "Sorry, Jenna, I'm going to have to call you later."

"Susan? Gorgeous? What's going on? Is that Marcus shouting? Tell me what's happening. Put me on loud speaker."

"N-n-no. I'm fine."

"Susan." Jenna was firm. "Put me on loud speaker."

Susan looked up at Marcus. "I'm putting Jenna on loudspeaker." She clicked the button and placed the phone back down on the counter.

"What's going on?" asked the echoing voice.

Marcus stepped in closer, angling his mouth towards the receiver. "Why do you always have to get involved? Everything was fine before you got involved. Susan was a wonderful woman. An upstanding member of society." He sneered. "Now look what you've turned her into."

"Marcus, what are you doing in Susan's room?"

Marcus ignored the question and looked at Susan. "I'm not talking to her. Switch her off."

"Don't you dare, Susan. Tell me what's going on."

Susan spoke loudly. "Marcus has seen the report. He doesn't want me to send it in."

Marcus looked back at the phone. "If she sends it in then I'll report her for leaving a young helpless child at the services on the ski trip that she was supposedly in charge of. I'll also report her for sending sexual images over the school's Wi-Fi."

The echoing voice was laughing. "You total tosser. *You* were also a teacher on that trip. They'll blame you too."

Marcus sniffed. "Fine, I'll just tell them about the sex shots you've been sending each other then."

"He saw my laptop," said Susan.

Jenna was still laughing. "Oh you total tosser. Just tell him to do one, Susan."

"She's not that silly," said Marcus. "Are you, my mon amie?"

"Marcus, I'd like you to leave."

"Not until you tell me you're adding some positives to that report."

Susan gasped. "I've already taken out the negatives!"

"You've what?" shouted the voice from the phone. "I hope you haven't taken out the negatives!"

"What negatives?" said Marcus.

"I've taken out all of the bits about you pursuing me."

"Pursuing you?" Marcus scoffed.

"The way you'll touch my leg as you're talking to me. Or the way you tried to touch my breasts when we took that ski trip photo."

"I did no such thing! And as for touching your leg, well that's simply a tactile gesture between friends." He lifted his nose and looked at Susan in disgust. "I'm a taken man, Susan. Angel and I are official."

"Marcus!" Jenna was loud. "Listen very carefully. You leave that room right now. You leave that room knowing that Susan *will* be including those facts. You leave that room knowing that I will also be writing a report, and I'll be sending it to Vice Principal Brown first thing in the morning. You called my colleague Amber a social misfit. You were rude to my instructor Lisa. I heard you questioning why any red-blooded male would fancy an albino. You were offensive about my sexuality. You—"

"Jenna, stop, it's fine." Susan's voice was shaking. "I can handle this."

"You can't, Susan! You need support! I'll support you. I'll send in a report. I'll cite all of his snivelling, sarcastic comments and his inappropriate—"

"Jenna, please. I've got this under control."

Marcus glanced at his colleague. "Mon amie?"

"I'd like you to leave."

"And you'll make the right choice if I do?" He lowered his voice. "You'll take control of this, umm," he nodded at the phone, "this, umm, situation as well?"

"I'd like you to leave."

Susan watched as Marcus slowly retreated out of the room, nodding at her and giving her an apprehensive thumbs up as he left, quietly closing the door behind him. She quickly dashed to the door and locked it, picking up her phone from the counter and turning off the loudspeaker. She rushed to her bed and sat down, keeping her voice quiet. "Jenna? Jenna, are you still there? He saw the photos. He saw all of them."

Jenna's voice was controlled. "What a total little fucker."

"He saw the photos!"

"So?"

"So he saw them! He'll tell."

"Who will he tell? What will he tell? Calm down, Susan, you've got nothing to worry about."

"Jenna, you told me this was safe!"

"I didn't know he'd walk in. He might have seen the photos but he's not got copies of them. What are you worrying about?"

"I knew this was a bad idea. I should have gone with my instinct."

"Hey, I didn't ask you to unbutton your blouse. I didn't ask you to straddle your screen."

"But you encouraged me to do it. I get carried away with you."

Jenna was silent for a moment. "I don't think that's totally fair."

"But he's right. I'm on the school site."

"No, you're in your own private apartment in the staff living quarters, and anyway, you use a dongle don't you? You're not even on the school's Wi-Fi. You're on your own 3G."

Susan rubbed her temples. "You can't try and justify my behaviour to me."

"So you didn't enjoy it then? You weren't having fun?" Jenna lowered her voice. "I'd like to carry on that fun if you would? Didn't you see my last few pictures? I got myself so close."

"Jenna! How can you even suggest that! Don't you care about what's gone on?"

"What? He's being a tosser. Ignore him."

"How can I? He's threatening me."

"With what? He won't tell them about Daisy, and he certainly won't tell them about the pictures."

"He might."

"He won't!"

"Why not?"

"He's got no proof."

****

Marcus scurried down the hall and pushed open the double doors, crossing the pebble path from Susan's block to his own. He dashed back into the warmth of the corridor and fumbled in his pocket for his room key, reaching his door and getting inside as quickly as he could. He grabbed his laptop from his messy kitchen counter that was strewn with unwashed plates and half empty coffee cups, and sat down on the sofa, flipping the lid and tapping his feet as he cursed the slow start up.

****

"What if he tries to get proof, Jenna? What if he tries to pull me down with him?"

"How would he get proof? I think you should just calm—"

"From Skype! You might be fine sending naked images across the World Wide Web, but I'm not."

"What?"

"It's true. You've done this before. I haven't. Do you realise how humiliated I feel?"

"What makes you think I've done this before?"

"Jenna, you've done everything before." Susan gasped. "You don't even care that you're all over Facebook. You've made things a thousand times worse with Marcus! He'll definitely try and get some evidence against me now he thinks you're writing a report."

"I am."

Susan was shaking her head. "You're not. And I'm sending mine in exactly as it is, with the facts, just the facts."

"Susan, his behaviour's inappropriate. His behaviour with you this afternoon has been inappropriate."

"No, *my* behaviour's inappropriate."

"You Skyped your girlfriend. What's the big deal?"

"On the school site."

"In your personal apartment. Susan, really, what's the big deal?"

Susan shook her head and jumped off the bed. "I need to delete Skype. I need to delete it off my laptop."

****

Marcus scrolled as quickly as he could to the Skype app. He'd never opened it before and wasn't quite sure what to expect. He pushed his

108

glasses further up his nose as he stared at the screen. *Looks pretty simple,* he said to himself as he entered the username: **Susan.Quinn**

****

"Don't be so silly," said Jenna. "You don't need to delete the app. We talk on it every day."

"Well maybe we shouldn't." Susan was back on the bed with her laptop on her knee.

"Argh! Susan will you please just calm down! Let me talk you through deleting the conversation. It's really simple." Jenna sighed. "We can't not have our afternoon Skype sessions."

"And it'll disappear? All of it?" Susan scrolled through the string of messages and pictures, cursing her own stupidity.

"All of it," said Jenna.

****

Marcus pursed his lips. **JennaJames**. The red box flashed up. Incorrect password. He tried again. **JamesJenna**. Same box. He thought carefully. Maybe Susan set up Skype before the ski trip. Maybe the password was old. He clicked back on the box and typed the word: **Teacher**. "Damn," he muttered as the access was denied. Marcus leaned backwards on the sofa and stared at the ceiling, desperately trying to wrack his brains. All he needed was a tad more leverage for Susan to be on his side. She'd vouch for him. She'd silence the critics. He smirked to himself. Pornographic pictures would provide the perfect leverage. **StWilfreds**, he typed, shooting off the sofa as the access was granted. He swept his arm across the counter, chinking the cups together and clearing some space. He placed the laptop down and jumped onto the stool, moving as close as he could to the screen.

His moan was deep, guttural, and full of pleasure.

****

"Click on *tools*."

Susan nodded. "Okay."

"Click on *options*."

"Okay."

"Click on *privacy*."

"Okay."
"Now you'll see there's a button on the right that says *clear history.*"
Susan nodded. "I see it."
"So clear your history."

****

Marcus wiped a spot of drool from the corner of his mouth. "*You dirty, dirty—*" He stopped suddenly and sat backwards on his stool. He stared at the screen and tapped the keypad. "*What? Where did that go?*" He scrolled up and down but saw nothing. "*No!*" he gasped, logging out and then back in again. He clicked from tab to tab to tab searching for the string of messages. "*No!*" he cried. "*It's gone!*"

CHAPTER SIXTEEN

Susan entered the large oak office on command. It was 6.30 p.m. and Dorothy Brown had left her waiting in the corridor like a naughty school girl, punishing her for not disclosing Marcus's altercation with Daisy Button at the very first opportunity. She glanced out of the large sash window across the dark acre, eyes drawn to the floodlit pitches in the distance. It was cold, dank and Susan couldn't wait for the day to be over. She stood still in the designated spot, three feet away from the desk.

"That's the report?" Dorothy Brown was pointing at the piece of A4 paper that Susan had been clutching in the corridor for the past half hour.

"Yes." She stepped forward and handed it over before returning to her spot.

Dorothy Brown flapped the thin sheet. "Is this it?"

"The three headings you asked for, with facts."

Dorothy huffed and lifted her glasses from the desk, hmm-ing at different points in the text. "Short, but informative," she said, finally placing the piece of paper back down. "Now tell me. More importantly. How did he behave with Willamena Edgington?"

"Willamena?" Susan paused. "He was fine, I think. Nothing unprofessional that I was aware of." She shook her head. "No, there was nothing that I'd add to the report."

"Nothing?"

Susan shook her head. "Nothing I noticed."

"Aha, so there could have been something?"

"No, I didn't mean that."

"But you admit you weren't paying attention to the pair of them. There could have been something."

"No I don't think so."

"Thinking's not good enough. You have to know." Dorothy Brown took off her glasses and nodded. "I'll add you to the list."

111

Susan sounded almost apologetic. "What list?"

"Professor Ramsbottom's being investigated, and I do believe we have enough evidence to warrant a tribunal." She tapped Susan's report. "You're not the only witness who's been fact finding. I've had reams from his head of department, and his head of house couldn't file her report fast enough. Not to mention parental complaints and criticism."

"Will it be an official tribunal?"

Dorothy Brown cleared her throat. "Principal Cavanagh is letting me take the lead on this one. She's utilising my years of experience. I think I'll keep it all 'in house' to start with. You know how crippling bad publicity can be for an establishment like ours." Dorothy shook her jowls. "But if he doesn't jump ship of his own accord then I'll be more than happy to escalate."

Susan glanced back across the acre and stayed silent.

"So," said Dorothy with gusto, "until the tribunal."

"Will I be needed?"

"Madam Quinn, you'll be instrumental. You'll testify against him. You'll tell the panel all about his sexual harassment and inappropriate behaviour." She flapped the report once more. "It's all in here. There's no going back now."

"I, umm, I don't think I mentioned the term sexual harassment, did I?"

"No need." She nodded. "This speaks for itself."

****

Susan walked slowly back to her room, unable to decide if Marcus was right in his accusation of Dorothy Brown's personal vendetta, or if he was, in fact, in need of a professional warning and possible suspension. She shook her head. Marcus was just being Marcus, wasn't he? She paused. But what if there *was* something untoward happening between him and Willamena? She nodded. She was only sixteen. That *would* be cause for a tribunal. Susan shook her head again. No, of course nothing was happening between them. She was smart. Sensible.

"Madam Quinn, are you having another one of your fits?" The voice was giggling.

Susan turned around. "Oh, hi girls."

It was Champagne's turn to laugh this time. "We've been following you down the corridor and your head's been wobbling around like Churchill the nodding dog."

"Oh."

Champagne pulled up alongside her teacher. "Are you okay? Are you still worrying about Jenna? I can show you those pictures now if you want? We were just heading down to the video room for our Edward and Bella fix."

"No, it's fine. I'm fine. What's happened to Mischa and Phats?"

Champagne laughed. "Twilight."

Priggy stepped in closer. "Twilight last night, New Moon tonight, Eclipse tomorrow, and on Saturday night they're letting us watch both Breaking Dawns."

"You've lost me."

"Come with us," said Priggy, smiling. "I can't remember the last time I saw you in the video room."

Champagne rattled the packets of popcorn. "We've brought snacks."

Priggy patted the pink pillows under her arms. "And pillows."

Champagne pushed her friend's shoulder. "Susie's not going to be snuggling up with you, Priggs."

"She might!"

"I won't, and it's Madam Quinn please, girls."

"Are you sure you're okay?" asked Champagne. "I think I'm going to message Jenna and tell her to start her training early. You need her back here. It's obvious."

Susan frowned. "You're in contact with Jenna?"

"Of course. She's hilarious on WhatsApp, isn't she Priggs?"

"Hilarious!"

Susan sighed. "Have fun at the film, girls. I'll see you in class."

Priggy wiggled her pillow once more. "Are you sure we can't tempt you? I spray perfume on my pillow."

"No," said Susan, turning the corner and walking away from them, down the wide oak corridor towards the staff living quarters. She picked up her pace as she pushed through the double doors that lead to the student dorms, deliberately keeping her head low until she got to the safety of the 'staff only' section of the block.

"Ah! Mon amie, I've been looking for you."

"Oh what now?!" snapped Susan.

"Temper, temper."

"It's been a long day. I'm heading back to my room."

Marcus lifted the corner of his moustache into a lopsided grin. "All of your extra-curricular activities no doubt."

Susan glanced over her shoulder to check that the doors had closed behind her. "Never discuss this with me again."

"Can I discuss it with others?"

"There's nothing to discuss."

"I'll tell you what," said Marcus rubbing the corners of his mouth with his fingers, "I'll make you a deal. You stay quiet about me and I'll stay quiet about you."

"Marcus, I've handed in the report."

"What? You haven't? As it was?"

"As it was."

"And Jenna? Is she sealing my fate too?"

Susan shook her head. "I don't know, Marcus. But this is much bigger than Jenna and I."

"What do you mean?"

"Dorothy has reports from your head of department *and* your head of house. She also says she's received parental complaints."

"Complaints?"

"Yes, complaints."

"Plural? I know about the ridiculous one from Willamena's parents, but she's bluffing if she says there are more."

"She didn't name names." Susan paused. "But there'll be a tribunal."

"Oh don't talk such nonsense. She'll wheel old Martha Adams and Mary Llewellyn into some class room and get them to listen to all of your claptrap." Marcus fingered his thinning hair. "Teachers get suspended instantly if they're accused of malpractice. I wouldn't be here if they'd found anything."

Susan frowned. "Is there anything to find?"

"No, of course not." Marcus tried to smile. "But I need your support, Susan. We could be one another's defence council."

"I don't need a defence council. I've done nothing wrong." Susan tried to walk off.

"You're into more mischief than me, Susan." Marcus was back at her side matching her pace.

Susan kept her eyes forward. "What I do in my own time is my own business."

"On the school site. On the school Wi-Fi."

Susan upped her pace. "In my own apartment. On my own Skype. With my own webcam."

Marcus stopped suddenly, letting Susan walk away, as an image of a pork chop flashed into mind. *You had two apps open,* he thought. *You minimised your webcam first.*

CHAPTER SEVENTEEN

Jenna sat down in a booth near the back of the cocktail bar. It was Thirsty Thursdays and the place was rammed, mostly due to the offer of a free fishbowl with every round of drinks that came to more than twenty euros. She dropped the change into Hugo's hat, which was sitting in the centre of the table and acting as the makeshift kitty. They had all added forty euros and knew they would be set for the night ahead.

"What have we got coming?" asked Amber.

Jenna grinned. "Four Jägerbombs, four bottles of Bud, and a cheeky vimto fishbowl."

Lisa looked shocked. "And you still got change from a twenty?"

"Yes. Lyndsey's behind the bar."

"You dirty dog," laughed Amber, narrowing her eyes and fingering her tall pink hair. "Are you still seeing her?"

Jenna shook her head. "Of course not. She's a friend." She paused as she handed out the long twisting straws. "I'm happily taken."

Hugo spoke in his strong French accent. "I am unsure if everyone knows of zis." He nodded at Lyndsey who was making her way over with the huge tray of drinks. "I 'ave just been watching 'er applying 'er lipstick and 'er, 'ow you say it? Bloosher? Behind zee bar."

"She hasn't," laughed Jenna.

"She 'as," nodded Hugo as Lyndsey arrived at the table.

Jenna looked up and smiled at the freshly painted face. "Thanks, Lynds. That's great. Looks like you'll be run off your feet tonight."

"Oh you know me, calm in a crisis. I'll still have enough energy to hit a club after my shift if you fancy it? Or maybe we could just go for a coffee in that late night bar back in Morzine? You might need sobering up after all of these fishbowls?" She smiled and pulled her long hair back behind her ear. "Or maybe you'll want to continue the fun somewhere else?"

Jenna sensed the silence coming from her booth. All eyes and ears were on her. "Ah, thanks, Lynds, but I don't think it's going to be a late one."

"Yes it is!" said Amber. "This lot are back on the schools with me next week, so they're making the most of their current chalet schedule."

"Maybe catch you later then?" said Lyndsey, looking at Jenna.

"Okay, maybe," said Jenna with a nod.

The group waited for the barmaid to disappear into the pack of après skiers, before directing their laughter and comments at Jenna. "You're so bad," said Lisa.

"I'm not!"

"You are," laughed Amber. "You just can't say no, can you? I could have been offering myself out on a plate and she'd still only have eyes for you."

Jenna shook her head. "I just don't like being mean to people."

"Sorry, I've got a girlfriend, isn't mean," said Lisa, lifting her straw to the purple coloured bowl.

"But she'd think I was presuming something if I said that. She's a friend, that's all."

"A friend you've fucked," added Amber.

"Zee lady likes you."

"Oh stop it you lot," said Jenna, adding her straw to the bowl, immediately responsible for the sudden drop in liquid height.

"Games, games, games," said Hugo tapping his hands on the table. "Can we do zat ducky fuzzy one?"

"Fuzzy duck?"

"Zat one! Oui!" said Hugo, displaying his brilliant white smile. "I start. To my left, fuzzy duck."

Amber quickly swallowed her mouthful. "Fuzzy duck."

"Fuzzy duck," said Lisa.

"Does he?" asked Jenna, sending the game back in the opposite direction.

Lisa grinned. "Ducky fuzz."

"Ducky fuzz," said Amber.

Hugo nodded. "Ducky fuzz."

"Does he?" asked Jenna, once again changing direction.

"Fuck a duck," said Hugo, before bursting into laughter. "Zat is not fair. You always just say does he!"

Jenna smiled. "Anyone can say it. You're getting better though. Let's go again. To my right."

"Wait!" Hugo was beaming once more. "Henri, Henri!"

Jenna turned around and saw Hugo's boyfriend edging his way through the mix of people, some of whom were still dressed in ski jackets and salopettes, having come straight from the slopes, and others who were dressed more smartly for a night on the tiles. "Hey," she said with a wave, to the perfectly preened French man.

"Henri!" giggled Hugo, quickly plumping up his perfect black quiff and rubbing his tongue across his teeth. "Que faites-vous ici?"

Henri smiled at the group, "Bonsoir, everyone," before directing his attention to Hugo. "Changement de plan. Pas de travail."

"Come join us," said Hugo with his hands outstretched.

Henri looked at the mass of drinks littering the table and pursed his mouth. "Non merci. Je tiens à vous prendre pour un restaurant."

Hugo glanced nervously around the group. "Umm."

"Go!" said the girls, all having a good enough grasp of French to know that Henri would rather wine and dine his partner than stay and drink like a fish while he fucked a duck.

"Really?" asked Hugo, already tipping the notes and change out of his hat and onto the table.

"Désolé, Mesdames. I just love my man."

"Now that's how you do it," said Amber, nodding at Jenna.

"Susan's not here!" said Jenna. "But if she were here then I'd be wining and dining her too. At a restaurant. A posh restaurant, with a pianist and a price tag to match." She stood up and let Hugo slide out of the booth.

"No you wouldn't," said Lisa, sharing out Hugo's drinks, "you'd be dragging her out with us."

"Bye guys," said Hugo and Henri, holding hands as they turned around to make their way through the crowd of people.

"Bye."

"Bye."

"Have fun!" said Jenna, immediately turning back to her colleagues. "No I wouldn't."

"You would!" Amber laughed. "Remember that time you had that girlfriend for a week. You kept getting us to accidentally bump into you so we could turn it into a group night out instead."

"But she wasn't Susan. Susan's special."

Amber smirked. "You can say that again."

"Hey, I liked Susan," said Lisa. "Do you think you'll see her again?"

"She's my girlfriend! Of course I'll see her again!"

Lisa sucked on her straw, watching the purple liquid wind its way around loop after loop before finally reaching her lips. She swallowed quickly and bowed her head, ready for another go. "But she's in a different country."

"And I'll be there in three months too."

Amber reached for Hugo's bottle of Bud. "Three months is like a lifetime in lesbian lovers for you. Why don't you just put her out of her misery and end things now?"

"This is love! I'm in love!"

"Oh no," laughed Lisa, "not another evening of you declaring how you'd catch a grenade for her."

Jenna started to sing. "I'd throw my hand on a blade for her."

"Enough!" shouted Amber.

"I'd jump in front of a train for her."

Lisa was giggling. "Okay, we get it."

Jenna paused. "So leave me alone!" She grinned. "Or I'll bore you with a long list of her good points. She ticks every single box, she really does."

Amber grimaced. "I can't quite imagine that's true."

"It is! She's perfect. I've honestly found the perfect woman."

Amber folded her arms. "Sexually." She grimaced again. "You can't possibly tell me that that nerdy teacher from three weeks ago with that Cotton Traders fleece and flat hair, is some kind of crazy cat in bed."

Jenna laughed. "She is. She's a crazy cat."

"You lesbians confuse me," said Lisa, shaking her head.

"I'm not a lesbian," corrected Amber.

"Okay, but you were."

"No, I dabbled, but the dramatics annoyed me." She glared at Jenna. "Men are much simpler creatures."

Lisa nodded. "Okay, so you're greedy, but still." She took a long slurp of drink. "My point is, how can she be crazy? How can anything be crazy when there are no trains and tunnels involved?"

Jenna laughed. "Having a tunnel's nothing to be proud of." She brought her hands together and made an echoing sound. "*Echo, echo, echo, echo.*"

Lisa reached out and hit Jenna on the arm. "You know what I mean. Sometimes the train can enter from the back, sometimes the front. I guess it can enter from all sorts of angles." She smiled. "Sometimes the train can even take a detour and silence the squealing."

Amber pulled a face. "What are you talking about?"

"Blow jobs," said Jenna. "Lisa here thinks us lesbians can't do positions because we don't have the hotdog to fill the bun."

"What?"

Jenna shrugged. "The boat to moor in the dock."

"The what?"

Jenna laughed. "The disk for the hard drive."

"I've got a laptop."

"Oh Amber! She's asking us what we do."

Amber looked at Jenna and smirked. "What *we* do? Now that *would* be telling."

Lisa lifted her eyes to her colleagues. "Are you two still?"

"No!" gasped Jenna.

Amber moaned. "But if we were we'd be kissing and cupping, and licking and sucking, and touching and teasing, and squeezing and pleasing. Not to mention all the pulling and grabbing, and thrusting and slamming, and—"

"Whoa, stop!" shouted Lisa. "Thrusting? Yeah right. With what?"

Amber nodded towards the fishbowl at Jenna's fingers. "She's very skilled."

"I'm just going to sit and drink until you've finished," said Jenna, tightening her grip around the curved glass.

"But they're fingers!" said Lisa. "It's not like she's got a huge penis pushing out of her peter pointer."

Amber nodded again. "Look how delicate they are." She nodded under the table at Lisa's legs. "Think how delicate *you* are. She's like a professional pianist playing a calming concerto that builds beautifully into a crashing climactic crescendo at the end." Amber took a swig of her beer. "And if you want your tunnel filled you just turn out the toys. Dildos, vibrators, strap-ons, plugs, balls, eggs, wands—"

"Stop!" said Jenna, "I can't drink anymore."

"It's true though," nodded Amber, "lesbians have the best of both worlds. They get the delicate fingers that actually know where they're going and what they're doing, and they also get the choice of internal implement." She shrugged. "Not like you straight women who get a bloke and a cock."

Jenna laughed. "You said *you* were straight."

"Why would anyone be straight when you spin it like that?" said Lisa. "Go and call her back, Jenna. Have some fun while you can!"

"How many times do I need to say this? I'm in love. I've found the one. I'm behaving!"

Amber scrunched up her nose. "You've hardly been tested, Jenna."

"I know," said Lisa. "What happens when you're cornered by some hot blonde?"

"Yeah," added Amber, lifting her leg under the table and moving it between Jenna's thighs. "What happens if you can't resist?"

Lisa carried on. "You can't resist the hot blonde who's clearly on a mission to find you."

Amber leaned her chest over the table. "What about the pink haired rep, who's after a re-run?"

"The blonde who's—"

"Stop saying blonde!" snapped Amber, dropping back down into her seat.

"But she *is* blonde," said Lisa, "and she's looking for you."

Jenna frowned. "Who?"

"Yep," nodded Lisa, raising her hand, "and she's seen you."

Jenna turned around and watched Jade, flanked by the three male execs, making her way to their table. "Hey," said Jenna as they approached. "How are you guys? I thought you were out in Morzine tonight?"

Bill, the eldest of the group spoke up. "Jade insisted we tried Les Gets, and I must say it's jolly lively over here. We've moved from bar to bar to bar."

"Come join us," said Amber with a smile.

"No, they've probably got other plans, especially if they're doing a bar crawl."

"Thirsty Thursdays at a cocktail bar?" Jade was nodding approvingly. "I'm not sure we'll find any need to move on from here. Shall I get us some drinks? They're bound to have Dom Perignon."

Bill patted the breast pocket of his jacket. "My round. I'll get us a couple of bottles. Is Champagne okay for everyone?"

Lisa and Amber sat up taller in their seats, discreetly trying to distance themselves from the purple coloured fishbowl. "Yes perfect, thank you."

Amber looked at the two younger men. "What type of execs are you?"

"We're bankers," they said in unison.

Lisa and Amber shared a glance. "We're single."

Jenna sighed. "Shall I finish the fishbowl then?"

"I'll give you a hand with that," said Jade, edging into the booth and forcing Jenna into Hugo's seat against the wall. Jade smiled and looked up at her colleagues. "Pete, Paul." She nodded towards the booth opposite. "It looks like they're leaving. There won't be enough room in here for us all. Grab it if you can."

The two young men turned around and secured the booth. "Are you ladies joining us?" they shouted to Lisa and Amber, who were already clambering out of their seats.

"You bet!" giggled Lisa.

The men nodded at their colleague. "You can stay where you are, Jade. We'll wave at you from a distance."

"With pleasure," said Jade, twisting around in her seat and facing Jenna. "You don't mind, do you? I could do with some peace and quiet."

Jenna heard the over-the-top flirtatious laughter of her friends, and smiled. "You know what, I don't."

"And here we go." Bill was back at the table with the two large bottles. "Oh. Where are they?"

Jade pointed towards the foursome.

"Oh, right. I'll, err, I'll drop off a bottle. That lovely barmaid said she'd bring over the glasses." Bill turned on his heels and took the Dom Perignon to the booth opposite. He returned and glanced down at the girls. "Should I slip in here, or should I add a chair to their table? What a quandary."

Jenna nodded to the empty bench recently vacated by Amber and Lisa. "Sit down, Bill."

"You ladies don't want an old fuddy duddy like me spoiling your giggles, and they certainly don't want a distraction to their wooing rituals." He placed the second bottle down on the table. "No. It's decided. I'm going to meander my way back to Morzine and take in the stars."

"Sit down, Bill," said Jenna.

"No. I'm bidding my leave." He reached back into the breast pocket of his jacket and removed his wallet. "Just make sure you have a great night," he said, placing two hundred euro notes on the table.

"Bill, there's no need," said Jade.

"I insist. Enjoy."

"No, Bill." Jenna watched as the older man crossed the room and said his goodbyes to the booth opposite. She also watched the way Amber picked up the hundred euro notes that he'd placed on their table too. She was tilting them in the light and gasping. Jenna frowned. "Why's he left us all so much money?"

Jade shrugged. "We'll want another bottle, no doubt. But it's embarrassing really. I earn double his salary."

Jenna shunned the posh bottle of plonk and stuck her straw back in the fishbowl. "I'm training to be a teacher."

"No? Really?"

Jenna took a quick sip and nodded. "I've put in my application form for a school-based programme and I'm waiting to hear if I'm needed on interview."

"Is the salary good?"

"No clue," said Jenna, taking a longer sip and grimacing slightly, unable to stop her eyes from wandering back towards the expensive bottle.

"Doesn't that matter?"

"Not really," said Jenna, sitting up straighter and giving up on the toxic beverage. "If you enjoy your job then you never work a day in your life."

Jade looked confused. "I thought you enjoyed your job already? You're a wonderful ski rep."

"I do. I just think it's time for a change."

Jade lifted the bottle of Dom Perignon and started to pour. "Do you have much experience?"

"I teach kids all the time. Some start skiing at the age of three; then I have the sulky sixteen year olds, and the—"

"Yes but schools are different, aren't they? Doesn't your life suddenly become completely constricted?"

"I'm not sure. I just know I'm ready for something more serious. I always run stage school classes in the summer months, and that's pretty similar to what I'll be doing."

"You'll teach drama?"

Jenna nodded. "My degree's in drama. I got a first from Durham."

"A first from Durham? Wow. You could work in the city with me!"

"Not with a drama degree. What would I be? The evening entertainment for you lot when you sell some shares?"

"You could be *my* evening entertainment."

Jenna ignored the blue eyes that were twinkling in her direction. "It just feels right."

"It does, doesn't it?"

Jenna picked up one of the freshly poured glasses and took a swig, ready to recite a really bad joke. "Ooo," she said instead, "this is delicious."

Jade lifted up the other glass and offered it out as a toast. "I think you'll be a brilliant teacher."

"Really?"

Jade smiled. "Yes, really. You're a natural. None of my instructors have ever managed to sort out my strange left turns. But you spotted them and fixed them within the first hour."

"Just doing my job."

"I think it was the physical element of your instruction that helped. What's it called? Kinesthesiology? The way you held my hip as you twisted me round."

Jenna laughed and said it again. "Just doing my job."

"Well you do it really well." She moved in closer. "And I'd love some more instruction from you if there's any on offer."

"Skiing?"

"What's your second subject?"

"Glasses," said Lyndsey, slamming the tray on the table. "I take it our date's off later then?"

Jenna rolled her eyes. "Lyndsey, this is Jade: she's been in my ski group for the week. Jade, this is Lyndsey, a friend."

"A friend she's fucked," added Lyndsey, turning to her competition. "Seriously, you're better off leaving now. She's a player, and I for one don't like being played." She lifted the empty beer bottles off the table. "That's the last time I fill your fishbowl for free, Jenna James."

Jenna shook her head. "I'm sorry, but I didn't, it wasn't ..." She sighed as she watched the waitress walk back to the bar. "I didn't promise her a date."

"Hey, I'm pleased," said Jade. "You're a player. I like to play."

****

Amber stretched out her arm, angling her phone in the direction of the booth opposite. She took the shot and smiled. "All bets are on," she said, opening Facebook and posting the picture.

CHAPTER EIGHTEEN

Susan slumped down on her bed. Something was irritating her but she wasn't sure what. She closed her eyes and let out an elongated sigh. She knew what. It was Marcus and his non-stop badgering. It was Dorothy and her non-stop badgering. It was Priggy and Champagne and their non-stop— Susan stopped herself. She was missing Jenna. No matter how hard she tried, she just couldn't get things right. Jenna hadn't forced her to take the photos, and Jenna certainly didn't know that Marcus was going to barge in and see them. But yet she'd blamed her. She'd blamed Jenna. The person she was meant to love.

Susan opened her eyes and rubbed her temples. No one had told her it was going to be this hard. No one had prepared her for the anxieties, or the angst that other people's comments would cause. Priggy and Champagne were in contact with her girlfriend on WhatsApp. Why did that matter? Why did that bother her so much? Was it jealousy? Or was it the thought that Jenna still had parts of her life that were secret, closed off to her? Susan rolled her eyes at herself. It wasn't a secret. She probably had loads of people contacting her through numerous avenues both day and night. Jenna was allowed a life. Jenna was entitled to do as she pleased. Susan felt the emotion well up in her chest once again. *But Jenna's meant to be mine.* Why's she not asked me to join WhatsApp? She paused her thought and made a mental note to Google exactly what WhatsApp actually was.

Susan turned onto her side and reached across the bedside cabinet for her phone. She checked the time. It was only 9.00 p.m., 10.00 p.m. in Morzine: far too early to try to start a text conversation. She pulled the bed throw higher around her chest and scrolled through her apps, wondering whether to check the ski report or read the local Morzine news instead. She sighed at her own uselessness. She didn't really care that there had been fifteen centimetres of snowfall, or that eighty two of the eighty five ski lifts were open. She just knew she wanted to feel closer to Jenna. Susan checked the time once more. Their habit of late night texting tended to begin anywhere between midnight and 2.00 a.m. UK time, as soon as Jenna was home, safe, and settled in bed. Susan closed her eyes. She had three hours to wait. Often she'd drop off, relying on her loud message tone to wake her, thankful for the few hours' sleep she'd managed to get before their text chat began. Tonight, however, she felt restless. She adjusted her pillow and sat back up, swiping her phone to life once more. Maybe one little nose wouldn't matter. She looked down as her finger hovered over the app she'd promised she'd delete.

****

"So, show me once more," giggled Jade, "I've forgotten the snap."

"You haven't forgotten. Your left turns have been perfect all week."

Jade giggled again. "No, I seriously think I've forgotten. Finishing off this fishbowl has made me forget."

Jenna took a sip of Champagne. "I told you to leave it. This is so much better."

"No, I actually quite like the taste of this." She sucked the final drop from the long twisting straw. "And you're loving those bubbles, so it's worked out okay." She plumped up her pink lips. "It tastes like cordial, and I like trying new things. But stop changing the subject, you." She smiled and looked out from under her long eyelashes. "Seriously, I've forgotten. You're my instructor. It's your job to help me. What if I fall over tomorrow when I'm trying to turn left, all because you refused to remind me tonight?"

"Fine," said Jenna reaching her arm over Jade's shoulder and placing it at the top of her left thigh. "You're skiing, you're skiing, you're skiing, you need to turn left, your weight moves onto your right ski." She lifted the top of Jade's buttock. "And SNAP, you lift your left leg round."

****

Amber smiled from the booth opposite. "And snap to you too," she said, adding another caption.

****

Susan clicked on the Facebook app and scrolled to the search button at the top. She hadn't changed her photo, or added anything else to the site, and that, combined with her lack of friends, had made her profile a sorry state of affairs. She didn't mind though, as her sole purpose for accessing the site had been to spy. Susan had promised to delete it, more for her own sanity than anything else, but the temptation was always there. The temptation to search Jenna's friends and see what she could find. She was about to type in the name, Amber, when she noticed that her own white friends logo had suddenly turned red. She clicked on the link and studied the face that looked strangely familiar. Felicity Fenwick had requested her friendship. Susan found herself laughing out loud. Felicity Fenwick. Now she was a blast from the past. She had been in their class at St Wilfred's and was one of those girls who always managed to find trouble wherever she went. Whether she was adapting her uniform to shorten her skirt, or screaming like a cat every time the teacher turned to face the board, she got in trouble, simple as that. Susan smiled again. Her favourite memory of Felicity had been when she'd covered Battle-Axe Brown's car in bird seed in retaliation for a detention she didn't think she deserved. Needless to say the messy white splatterings left on the pristine paintwork were well worth the hour she'd spent in the library doing lines.

Susan clicked on the *accept friendship* button, immediately gaining access to Felicity's home page. She scrolled to the *About* section and read the facts. **Birthday:** July 11. **Gender:** Female. **Relationship status:** Single. **Interested in:** Women. Susan paused. Interested in women? Felicity was forever being found in the dorms of St Peter's All-Boys school down the road. How could she possibly like women? Susan smiled to herself, sure that Felicity would also find *her* new found interest in women just as amusing. She clicked on the photo tab and started to swipe. Felicity still had her trademark mischievous grin, and her flame-red hair was as wild as she remembered, but something was different. She had aged really well. Her features had flourished and she had blossomed into an exquisitely English-looking rose.

Susan glanced back up to her own profile picture that was sitting quietly in the corner of the screen. How embarrassing, she thought, cringing at the bowl haircut and badger jumper. She considered taking a quick selfie and updating the image, before remembering that Felicity would have seen her picture when she'd searched for her. Susan tapped on Felicity's friends button. Two hundred and thirty two friends. Why on earth had she felt the need to search for her, let alone add her? She moved to the timeline button, scanning over the posts and photos. Felicity Fenwick was clearly clever, popular and funny. Susan clicked play on a self-entitled 'Me Singing' video clip and watched with a smile as Felicity warbled her way through a unique version of *Let It Go* from the film *Frozen*, complete with dramatic arm actions and swooning facial expressions. Susan thought back to her own timeline, which was empty apart from her first three 'I'm lost, I don't know what to do on Facebook' posts. She sighed to herself. Maybe social media *was* the way forward. Maybe if she made herself look a bit more appealing, her friendship crisis would be over.

Susan scrolled back up to the search box and was about to type in Amber's name when her Facebook message symbol turned from white to red. This was a first. Susan clicked on the link a little too eagerly, somehow managing to hit the notifications button instead. No new notifications. Susan got herself back on track and clicked with nervous anticipation. Someone had messaged her. Someone had an important message for her, for Susan Quinn.

Quiffy Quinn? It said.

Susan felt mortified. No matter what she achieved in her life, that's what she'd be remembered for: an upside down quiff during her gymnastics lesson back in Year Nine. Susan dropped the phone onto the bed. Wasn't that rather rude? Messaging someone with an insult? How would Penelope Newman like it if she contacted her out of the blue saying: **What's up, crater face?** Or Janine Talbot being greeted with the words: **Long time, specky four eyes.** Susan thought for a moment. At least Felicity hadn't pretended to forget about the incident, just like Jenna had done. She picked up the phone and started to type. "Hello Felicity. Yes, I am the Susan Quinn you went to school with."

The response was almost immediate. **You haven't changed a bit. How's things? Not much on your profile.**

"That's an old picture. I've only just got back on Facebook. I'll add more stuff soon. How are you?"

Split up with my long term girlfriend. Moved back to the area. Trying to find my feet again. Heard you worked at the school so thought I'd look you up. (PS: Hope you're not too shocked by the girlfriend admission. If I'm honest I always had you down as a same-sex kind of gal, but checked your profile – it says you're interested in men.)

Susan frowned, vaguely remembering a list of basic information she had to fill in when she first joined. She started to type. "Not been on here for six years. Lots to change. Am actually in a relationship with Jenna James."

WHAT???

Susan smiled to herself and typed back. "What?"

THE Jenna James?

Susan attached a picture from her phone's camera roll of her and Jenna smiling in the snow. "This Jenna James?"

Wow! You look incredible. You were right! You have changed. Take that bloody badger picture down right now and get this one up! Flipping heck! I'd never have put you two together. But you look great. You both look really happy. Is she on Facebook?

"Thank you. No, she shies away from social media. Says there are too many skeletons in the closet."

Sounds about right. She was a naughty one!

"About as naughty as you."

Ha! Yes! I'd love to catch up with you guys. I've moved into the Westbury estate opposite the Black Bear. Shall we go for drinks?

"Jenna's actually a ski rep in France. She won't be back until the end of April."

Oh no, that must be tough for you. How long have you been together?

Susan thought it best to round up. "Almost a month."

Ha! And you're trusting her all alone for that amount of time? She MUST have changed too. I'd still like drinks with you though, if you're around.

Susan's banged out her reply: "I'll check my calendar and let you know," finding it very difficult not to add: "Nice chatting again, Fuck-Em-All Felicity." She dropped the phone onto the bed and rubbed her face. Why did people find it so difficult to believe that Jenna could be faithful? Didn't they think she was a big enough draw for her? Or was it Jenna's sexual appetite that was so off the scale that it was a physical impossibility for her to go longer than five seconds without sex?

Susan nodded to herself. Jenna was her girlfriend. Jenna had made her promises. Jenna had declared her love. She picked the phone back up. There was therefore no need to search for Amber's name and find out what Jenna had been up to. Susan sighed. She couldn't help herself. One little peep wouldn't matter. She started to type and clicked on the pink-haired jpeg that flashed up first, automatically scrolling to Amber's timeline.

Susan's stomach plunged in absolute panic. There were two pictures. Both of them tagged. The first was of Jenna, all cosy in a booth, with a blonde-haired lady. The second was still in the booth, but this time Jenna had her arm around the lady's back, and Jenna's hand was on her bottom. More painful though were the captions and comments. Everybody, it seemed, was placing a bet on how long it would take Jenna to succumb. Susan read and re-read. That was Jade. That was the lady who'd given Jenna her number.

Susan was frozen in panic. What should she do? What could she do? She tried to stay calm and see things from Jenna's point of view. Maybe Jade had trapped her arm as she was reaching out for the barmaid's attention. Maybe everyone else had nipped to the toilet. Maybe it wasn't even her Jenna after all. Susan lifted the phone back up. It was definitely her Jenna, and her Jenna's situation was compromising. Susan closed the Facebook app and opened her text messages. She clicked on Jenna's name and started to type. **Sorry for texting early. Just to let you know I'm feeling a bit tired. Are you still out?**

****

Jenna felt her phone vibrate in her pocket. She pulled it out and focused on the screen. "Sorry, I just need to reply to this," she said, quickly typing her response. **Everything okay? Still out, but won't be a late one I'm sure.**

Jade was leaning over her shoulder. "You're under the thumb, aren't you? This Susan's actually a secret stifle-er?"

"A stifle-er?"

"Yes, someone who stifles. You should never be in a relationship with someone who pulls you down or dampens your spirit. You need to be with someone who talks you up and enjoys your energy."

Jenna smiled. "Trust me. Susan enjoys my energy."

"You're such a tease."

"I'm not! But Susan's great. She's seriously great. Our relationship's fairly new and it's always better to reassure by replying as soon as possible."

"That sounds like it's coming from someone who's learned the hard way."

"I learn everything the hard way," laughed Jenna, putting her phone down and taking another sip of Champagne. "But I'm trying. I'm really trying. I love Susan and I want to get this right." Jenna paused. "She's my world. I honestly never thought I'd be able to say that about someone, but I can. Susan's my *absolute* world."

"But she's not here. She's not even close by." Jade lifted her hands. "Isn't this your world?" She turned her hands inwards. "Isn't this your here and now?"

"Jade, you're lovely, but—" Jenna lifted her phone as it vibrated once more. "Hang on."

"Mobiles make you miss moments," said Jade, looking up and pointing at all the people in the crowded bar. "See. There are phones everywhere. Heads are down and moments are missed."

"I'm just replying to my girlfriend," laughed Jenna, typing out her reply. "I'm hardly missing a monumental moment in the mountainous region of Morzine."

"We're in Les Gets!" Jade laughed. "See! You fiddle with your phone and your focus is fucked!"

Jenna grinned. "I'm good at focusing when I fiddle. Can we stop talking in rhymes now, and can you stop distracting me? Susan's asked why it won't be a late one, and if anyone's gone home, so I need to reply, and the sooner I reply, the sooner I'll be back in the room."

"You said it won't be a late one? Charming!"

"It won't. Now let me answer her so I can tease you with another tongue twister."

"Is that a promise?"

Jenna tapped quickly. **Hugo's gone, but Lisa and Amber are still here. Just not feeling it tonight.** Jenna nodded and pressed send. "There, no moments missed. I'm back in the room, ready to relish the random—"

"Stop! Your tongue twisters are as bad as your jokes." Jade reached for the phone and held it above her head. "You need distracting."

"Hey," said Jenna, looking up. "I don't need—"

"I'm down here," said Jade, lifting her lips onto Jenna's.

****

"And here we have it," said Amber, taking the final shot.

****

Susan read the message again. **Lisa and Amber.** No mention of Jade. She shook her head and opened the Facebook tab. Maybe they were in the background somewhere. Maybe she had missed them the first time round. She clicked back on Amber's page and shouted out with shock as her whole world came crashing down around her: the vision of Jenna's locked lips just too much to bear. She fumbled for her text message tab and typed through her angry tears: **Feel it as much as you like, because you're not feeling me anymore.**

CHAPTER NINETEEN

Susan closed the classroom door and began her final lesson of the day: Year Thirteen general studies. It was one of those additional A-Levels the school made everyone take to try to up their pass rate percentage. However, the fact it was 'additional' meant it always had the lowest lesson attendance rate, with students failing to see its value. Susan looked around the classroom. Only six or so of the twenty sixth form students had turned up, which disappointed her because she had been looking forward to teaching the lesson. In fact, she had been looking forward to teaching all of today's lessons until the events of last night put a severe dampener on things. She took a deep breath and tried her best to sound upbeat.

"Okay ladies, thank you for turning up. Today we're looking at behaviour and attitude. We're going to examine how they're formed and how they can be changed."

"Will this be in the exam?" asked Sunny Davis from the back of the room.

Susan put on her best acting voice. "Oh dear! You've just reminded me, Sunny. I've left the syllabus in my pigeon hole in the staffroom. Would you mind nipping out and fetching it for me please?"

"Haven't we got the syllabus already?"

"Yes, but I've printed off some more copies so we can highlight the elements of the course that are compulsory that will definitely come up in the exam, and those areas where you'll have a choice of topic."

Sunny was flicking through her folder. "Can't we just do that with the one we've already got?"

"If you don't mind, I'd like you to go and pick them up, please."

Sunny rolled her eyes and stood from her chair, slowly making her way out of the classroom. "Yes, Madam Quinn."

Susan waited for the door to close before racing to her desk. "Okay," she said, switching on the interactive whiteboard and opening her presentation, "we're playing a trick."

The girls in the class looked confused.

"I'm going to show you how easy it is to change someone's perception. Perception's linked to attitude and belief, and this starter activity should be a great lesson opener."

Some of the girls sat up in their seats.

"So, when Sunny comes back in I'm going to show you these pictures." Susan started to click through the photos on the whiteboard: some were of boxes, some were of triangles, and some were of straight lines and circles, but all of the shapes were different sizes. "I'm going to ask you to write down which is the biggest, or smallest." She pointed up at the shapes, clearly marked with A, B, or C. "However, if I ask you for the biggest, I want you to write down the letter of the smallest, or if I ask you for the smallest I want you to write down the letter of the biggest."

"Why?" asked Philomena from the front.

"Because it's obvious which one's the biggest. She'll see the biggest. She'll write down the biggest. However, I wonder what will happen when we go through the results and she hears all of you saying the letter B, when she's actually written down the letter C."

Philomena lifted her nose. "Sunny's an A-grade student, she's not going to fall for this."

"Fall for what?" asked Champagne as she pushed through the door with Priggy in tow.

"Oh girls, you're late. Sit down quickly please."

Priggy bustled her way to the front of the room. "We didn't know whether to come or not, but Champs thought we should just to see how you're doing." Priggy lowered her voice, "We've got a message from Jenna. She's desperate—"

"Girls, sit down quickly. You're going to ruin the lesson."

Champagne tutted at Priggy. "See, I told you she'd be stressed; she's obviously seen the pho—"

"Girls! Sit down and listen. We're playing a trick on Sunny." Susan refreshed the pictures on the interactive whiteboard. "I'm going to ask you questions about these shapes. I'm going to ask you to write down the letter of the biggest, the smallest, the tallest, the shortest, etcetera." She paused to make sure Priggy and Champagne were listening. "But I want you to write down the opposite letter instead."

"What's the opposite of A?" asked Priggy.

"No, if I ask for the tallest I want you to actually write down the shortest."

Champagne took her seat and turned to her friend. "She's lost it. I told you she'd lose it, didn't I?"

"If I ask you the smallest, you write down the biggest."

"Why are we doing this, Madam Quinn?" said Priggy.

"Because we're studying attitudes and beliefs, and how easy they are to change. Just stay quiet. Don't tell Sunny what I've asked you to—" Susan stopped as the door opened and Sunny re-entered to an eerie silence.

"Madam Llewellyn and Madam Adams were in the staffroom and neither of them could find the syllabus."

Susan tried to act once more. She looked up to the ceiling and sucked on her bottom lip. "Deary, deary me, now where could I have put them?"

Champagne whispered under her breath. "I told you she'd lose it."

Sunny folded her arms. "Do you want me look somewhere else?"

"No, they're not important. We can highlight the ones you've got in your folder."

"Didn't I say—"

"Anyway, take a seat, Sunny, we've got lots to do." Susan clapped her hands. "Something related to attitude and belief is perspective." She re-opened her PowerPoint presentation. "As a little starter activity I'd like you to grab a piece of rough paper and answer the following questions." She clicked to the first picture of three different sized triangles. "No talking, please. Just write down the letter of the smallest triangle."

Priggy scrunched up her face at Champagne. "The biggest?" she mouthed.

Champagne nodded, and glanced to the back, loving the idea she might get one up on the ever so perfect Sunny Davis.

Susan clicked through to the next picture of three different length straight lines. "Which line's the shortest?"

The class silently jotted down their answers as they were asked for the biggest square, the tallest rectangle, and the smallest circle.

"Okay," said Susan, turning off the whiteboard. "Let's quickly run through the answers. Philomena, number one. The smallest triangle?"

Philomena nodded. "B."

"Great, Champagne?"

"B."

"Priggy?"

"B."

Susan continued her questioning until it came to Sunny, who kept her hand on her piece of paper and said, "B."

"Brilliant," said Susan, "and number two, which was the shortest line?"

Philomena started again, leading the class in a chorus of Cs.

"C," said Sunny.

"Ha! This is brilliant," laughed Champagne.

"No it's not," said Sunny. "What are we even doing this for?"

"Let's just run through the final few answers. Did everyone get B for question three?"

Everyone nodded and Sunny stayed silent.

"C for four?" The same nods came back. "And A for five?"

"Five out of five," said Priggy, licking her finger and waving it through the air.

Susan sat down on her desk and tapped her teeth together. "Now, Sunny, we've all got a confession to make. We played a little trick on you."

"What?" The A-grade student didn't look happy.

"While you were out I asked the class to write down the wrong answers. I wanted to show them what a huge influence peer pressure was on attitude and behaviour."

Sunny's cheeks flared up with colour. "I knew that wasn't the smallest triangle!"

"Hey, Sunny, I knew you wouldn't mind playing along. You're bright enough to understand the bigger picture."

Champagne laughed. "But not bright enough to spot the smallest triangle."

Sunny screwed up her piece of paper. "Oh yeah, ha ha, joke's on me."

"No, girls, stop. I knew Sunny could handle this, and Sunny, just so you know, I've done this every year with my general studies classes, and every single time the same thing happens." She nodded. "Isn't it interesting? You saw the smallest triangle. It was obvious to you which the smallest triangle was. Yet you gave me the letter of the largest triangle instead."

"Yeah, only because everyone else said B."

"So, are attitudes based on the beliefs of others?"

Sunny shook her head. "No, it just crossed my mind that I might be wrong and I didn't want to look like an idiot."

Champagne whispered under her breath. "Unfortunately you look like one now."

"Oh shut up, Champagne. I'm going," said Sunny, standing from her desk.

"No, Sunny, don't. Can't you see how this highlights the effect that other people can have on your own personal perception and belief? Please stay." Susan lifted the pile of papers. "I was going to get you to answer this question. It's from last year's exam, all about how attitudes are formed and what you can do to change them."

Sunny threw her bag onto her shoulder and walked to the front. "I'll do it in the library," she said, taking a sheet.

Philomena stood up too. "I think that was a bit unfair, Madam Quinn. I'll do mine in the library too."

"Are we going?" asked the girls at the back.

Susan placed the question sheets down on the table at the front. "For goodness sake, girls. You're eighteen. There was no offense meant by this."

Priggy and Champagne watched as the scattering of girls came to the front to collect their sheet before leaving the room. They stayed seated in silence.

"You two might as well go."

"Bad day?" asked Champagne. "We thought that might be the case."

"Did you really have to tease her like that?"

Champagne shrugged. "I'd have given the answers I'd got written down if you played that trick on me."

"That's just the thing," said Susan, shaking her head, "you probably wouldn't."

"I would, and it's brought little miss sunshine down a peg or two."

"Right, come on girls, off you go. I'm going to finish some marking."

"No," said Priggy, standing up from her seat. "We only showed up because we've got a message from Jenna."

Susan ignored her. "Take a question sheet from the front and bring it back next lesson."

"She says you're not answering her calls."

"Come on girls, off you go."

Champagne stood up and placed her hands on her hips. "You were so cool on the ski trip. We were really close. What's happened?"

"I've remembered my priorities. That's what's happened. I'm your teacher and I would like you to take this question sheet away and answer it to the best of your ability. This could well come up on the exam again in May."

Priggy sighed. "She wasn't kissing that Jade woman."

"Girls, I'd like you to leave."

Priggy continued. "She wasn't. She's devastated. She just wants you to return her calls. I know the picture looks bad, and I was like OMG Champs, come and check this out when I saw it, but then when I looked closely it was exactly how Jenna said it was."

"I don't care what Jenna's been saying." Susan rubbed her temples. "Seriously girls, this isn't a discussion we're about to have."

"That Jade woman grabbed Jenna's phone. She was waving it above her head. That's when she planted a kiss on Jenna. I even messaged Lisa on Facebook and she says that's exactly how it happened."

"Lisa was there too?" Susan shook her head. "No. It doesn't matter. Come on, girls, your exams are around the corner; you need to show some focus."

"How can we change your mind?" asked Champagne nodding at the board. "What does that say? To change someone's attitude you need to create cognitive dissonance?" She pulled a face. "What does that mean?"

"It doesn't matter what it means. Come on, off you go."

Champagne shook her head. "I'm your student, you're my teacher. I'm asking you to explain how you can change someone's attitude."

"I like your thinking, Champs," said Priggy, not following at all.

Susan sighed and stood up. "Fine. To change someone's attitude you need to create cognitive dissonance. Now off you go."

"I don't understand. Give me an example."

Susan sighed. "Fine. Your attitude's based on three things. The cognitive: What you believe to be true."

Champagne nodded. "So you believe she kissed Jade. You believe she's been unfaithful."

Susan ignored the statement. "The affective: Your feelings."

Champagne nodded again. "You're hurt by this."

"And the behavioural: How you act."

Champagne lifted her hands in conclusion. "So you're ignoring her."

Susan continued. "To change someone's attitude you need to cause a mismatch in these three elements. For example the thirteen year old smoker who thinks smoking's okay. That's the cognitive. They like the taste and the way it makes them feel like a cool kid. That's the affective. And they smoke because their friends do. That's the behavioural. If you highlight the negative effects of smoking, and they suddenly understand how harmful it can be to their body, then you've created an imbalance in their attitude and they may no longer think it's cool and they might even stop doing it, especially if you can get their friends to stop doing it too."

"What?" said Priggy with her face all scrunched up. "I didn't know Jenna smoked."

"It's simple, Priggs. Susie thinks Jenna's been unfaithful. She feels hurt by this, so she ignores her. If we prove to her that Jenna hasn't been unfaithful, then we'll create cognitive dissonance and she won't feel hurt. Her attitude will change, and she'll start talking to her again."

"How are we going to do that?"

Champagne grabbed her friend's arm and pulled her towards the door. "We're not, Jenna is."

"Girls, wait, I'd really rather you didn't get in—"

"Dissonance!" shouted Champagne, opening the door. "You've taught it us now!"

Susan closed her eyes, waiting for the door to slam shut, and was startled by the sound of Marcus Ramsbottom's voice instead.

"And this is my colleague, Madam Quinn's class, or dare I say, lack of it. They've probably had enough, or staged a protest, or—"

"Can I help you?" asked Susan, suddenly noticing the dolled-up barmaid as well.

"My Angel has requested a tour of the school. I've got a free afternoon so I thought I'd do the honours." Marcus was wearing his best tweed jacket and matching bowtie.

Angel plumped up her hair and stretched her long nails out towards the room. "Oh wow. Tammy and Tanisha would love it here." She did an excited little jump. "How soon do you think we can get them in?"

"Step at a time, my Angel, step at a time."

"I'm sorry, I've got marking to do," said Susan, dropping her eyes to the desk.

Angel lowered her voice. "I'll do it," she whispered.

Marcus coughed. "Thank you, Madam Quinn. We'll be off."

Angel was nodding with excitement. "I'll do it. I'll be your Britney. I'll do it. It's worth it for all of this."

Marcus stepped behind the barmaid and tried to shunt her out of the room. "Off we go then," he said.

Angel sucked on her first finger and flicked her leg out behind her. "*Hit me baby one more time.* You want me to wear plaits as well?"

Susan looked up in shock. "Angel, are you ..." She realised she had no clue how to phrase it. "Has he asked you to ..."

Angel was wiggling as her singing got louder. "*Oh baby baby, how was I supposed to...*" She paused. "I'll wear a *really* short skirt."

Susan stood up. "Angel, could I have a word?"

"No time, no time," said Marcus. "We're off to see the theatre next."

"Ooo, you have a theatre?" giggled Angel, tottering out of the room of her own accord.

CHAPTER TWENTY

Susan walked into the fusty communal lounge. It was 5.30 p.m., well past her usual Skype time with Jenna. She had stayed in the classroom following her disastrous sixth form lesson, catching up on all of her marking, and even managing to finalise her lesson preparation for most of next week. She had spent time doing the little jobs as well, like writing Monday's date on the board, and opening all of the textbooks to the correct pages before stacking them into neat piles; neither of which were truly necessary, but she wanted to stay busy. She'd even wasted time watering the crispy brown pot plants on the window ledge in an attempt to avoid her phone. It hadn't worked though, and it became harder and harder to ignore the sorrowful selfies of Jenna holding up a card that said 'call me.' Or the full length versions of Blue's *Sorry Seems To Be The Hardest Word* that came warbling through on her voicemail. The tipping point had come when she'd opened a picture message of a love-heart sweetie that simply said: *Yours*. Susan had switched off her mobile and marched through the school, knowing that a new focus was needed quite quickly. She wasn't trying to punish Jenna. She just didn't know what to say. She didn't know what to feel.

Susan closed the lounge door behind her and tried not to breathe in the fusty odour. She traversed the clothes horses that were weighed down with sports kit and apologised to the room as she tripped over a large bag of netballs. Susan looked up and realised that Mel Copeland from PE, who was head back, eyes shut, in her usual spot, hadn't heard, let alone noticed. She regained her balance and said hello to Martha Adams and Mary Llewellyn, but neither looked up from their game of chess.

"Bon bon?" asked Danielle Watts.

Susan sat down next to the school nurse and declined. "Anything good on tonight?"

"Well, we've got Neighbours now, Home and Away next, Hollyoaks at six thirty, Emmerdale at seven, Corrie after that, followed by Eastenders, then Corrie again, then at nine it's Gogglebox, but I hate Friday nights as there's never anything on."

"When? At ten?"

"Yeah." Danielle bit into a large bar of Cadbury's Dairy Milk. "You'd think they'd show something funny like Friends. Friday nights were always about Friends. Why can't they make something good like that again?"

Susan nodded. "Friends was good."

Mary Llewellyn lifted her head. "You say you're seeing friends? At the Black Bear? Would you pick up Martha's Red Ruby again, dear? We've drunk the dam dry."

"No, I'm not—"

"That Sunny girl of yours was at the staffroom today sending me on a wild goose chase for some syllabus or something or other. I couldn't quite hear what she was asking for. So yes, a bottle of the port would be much appreciated."

"No I—"

"Had me rooting around in your pigeon hole and all sorts."

"She's not got her hearing aids in," whispered Danielle.

Martha added to the conversation. "And I'd like some of those long menthol cigarettes if she's got any."

"No, I'm not—"

"Take a twenty," said Mary, pulling her small leather purse out of her skirt pocket and throwing it over to Susan.

Susan missed the catch and rubbed her knee, picking up the purse and pulling open the zip. She looked at the array of shrapnel. "I'm not going to the Black Bear."

"You're going to the Black Bear? Yes. Take my purse, dear."

Danielle Watts let out a huge sigh. "I'll come up with you at ten if you like? There's nothing on TV after all."

"Honestly?" said Susan, smiling. "That's great. I was hoping to catch up with Angel actually, and I could really do with the walk."

Danielle threw a handful of Maltesers into her mouth. "No chance. Chuck over your keys, Martha," she shouted. "We'll take the scooter instead."

"I'm not the deaf one," said Martha, rubbing her ears. She pointed towards the red mobility scooter parked up in the corner of the room. "Keys are in the ignition."

"Who needs permission?" asked Mary. "I've already told you to use my purse."

"No, the girls are taking the scooter."

"What computer? Is that what's making the noise?"

Susan pulled herself out of her seat. "No, that's the phone. I'll get it."

"We're taking the scooter. To the Black Bear," said Danielle, pronouncing every word with loud clarity.

"I know, it was my idea," nodded Mary, dropping her head back down to the board.

Susan dodged the stack of lacrosse sticks and banged into the arm that was dangling down from the sofa. She apologised quickly, but realised that Mel Copeland hadn't even flinched. "*Phone, phone, phone,*" she said, lifting an array of sports kit from the counter at the back of the room.

"Hello," she said, finally finding the old-fashioned receiver.

"Hello, I'm trying to get hold of Susan Quinn."

"Hi, yes, it's Susan speaking."

"Susan, hi! The school's sent me from pillar to post. I've been in the library, the theatre, the sports hall. Sorry, anyway, hello! It's Lisa from Club Ski."

Susan felt her cheeks flare up. "Lisa, hi."

"I just wondered if I could have a quick chat about last night? Jenna's really upset that you think something might have gone on with her and—"

"Is she there?" Susan lowered her voice. "Did she ask you to call?"

"Yes."

"Oh for goodness sake. Tell her I'll Skype her in five minutes."

"Would you like me to be there too?"

Susan could feel her anger rising. "No, we'll be fine, thank you."

"Okay, well listen, nothing—"

"Nice hearing from you again, Lisa. Speak to you soon." Susan hung up the phone and turned back around expecting all eyes to be on her, but the only movement she spotted was Mel Copeland's mouth as it dropped a little bit wider. Susan looked at Danielle. "I'll be back in a bit."

Mary Llewellyn frowned. "You're taking a sh—"

"Back in a bit," said Susan even louder.

"She's sure come out of her shell," said Mary, lifting her Queen and dropping it down to the kill square. "And that's checkmate."

****

143

Susan strode out of the lounge in a foul mood. How dare Jenna involve other people? How dare other people call her up at her place of work? How embarrassing that everyone had heard. Susan twisted her key in the lock and corrected herself. No one had heard, but still. It was inappropriate. This whole thing was inappropriate. She pushed open the door to her apartment and walked towards the counter in the centre of the room, lifting her laptop lid and taking a seat on the tall stool. Jenna had gone too far this time. Jenna would have to understand. This couldn't go on. This had to stop. She clicked on the Skype app and scrolled to Jenna's jpeg with the simple intention of hitting the green button and connecting the call. Instead she stopped, feeling her heart melt with instant warmth. Jenna had updated her profile image. The shot had been taken really close to the screen, and her big brown eyes were wide. A small word had been written on the top of her left cheek. *Sorry*, it said with two teardrops drawn underneath. Susan stared at the look of sadness and was overcome with emotion. Jenna was Jenna. She'd never change. But she loved her. She loved her for who she was.

Susan clicked on the image and waited. "Hey," she said as the connection came into focus, immediately laughing at the new word Jenna had printed on her face.

"Hey," said Jenna, ignoring the fact she had KNOBBER written across her forehead.

"Eyeliner?" asked Susan.

"Permanent marker."

Susan laughed. "No it's not."

"Maybe it should be," said Jenna. "I'm sorry. I'm so so so so sorry."

"What are you sorry for?"

"I'm sorry that you saw the photo. I'm sorry that Amber uploaded the photo. I'm sorry that I didn't mention Jade when I told you who I was out with. I'm sorry that I've bombarded you with photos and texts," she smiled, "and singing. But I guess I'm most sorry that you've lost your trust in me."

"Are you sorry for kissing her?"

"Susan, I tried to tell you last night. I tried to get Lisa to tell you today. I didn't kiss her. She kissed me."

"Is there a difference?"

"Of course there is. Ask Lisa, she was there."

"Well she wasn't, was she? It was just you and Jade in that cosy little booth."

"Jade's fine. She's harmless."

Susan shook her head. "You said that about Amber. These women aren't harmless, Jenna. You just don't see what other people see in you, do you? You give off vibes. You must do."

"I don't mean to."

"But you do."

"I'm sorry."

Susan wasn't ready to accept any apologies yet, so she carried on. "And how exactly did you end up in a booth all by yourself, with a blonde lady attached to your lips?"

Jenna sighed. "I've been teaching her all week. She was fine with me today. They leave tomorrow. I won't be seeing her again."

"But there'll be someone else next week, and the week after that. People want you, Jenna. They'll always want you."

"The only person I want to want me is you."

Susan stared at the wide eyes. "Lying by omission is still lying."

"I didn't mention Jade because she'd only just arrived. I was trying to protect you. To reassure you." Jenna shook her head. "I was never *meant* to be out with her. She just turned up."

"Yes, she turned up to see you, no doubt."

"Maybe."

"And you couldn't tell her to leave?"

"No. I'm her ski rep."

"And that means you have to kiss her?"

"She kissed me."

"There's no difference."

"Of course there is."

Susan reached out and adjusted her laptop screen. "You must have given off signals. People don't just kiss you for no good reason. You must have encouraged her."

"I didn't."

"But you probably did." Susan nodded. "It happens all the time. You just don't realise it. You're charismatic, Jenna. People love being around you. They want to get close to you. You draw them in."

"I'm sorry."

Susan paused. What was she cross at? What was the issue here? She sighed and shook her head knowing the truth. "I'm jealous."

Jenna frowned. "What of?"

"Everyone."

"But I'm yours."

"You're not."

Jenna nodded. "I am. I'm yours."

"Oh Jenna, I'm just finding this really hard. I—" Susan stopped as she heard the shouting.

"YO YO YO! It's party time! Oh hey, Susie," said Amber, suddenly appearing in the screen.

Susan watched as the pink-haired ski rep laughed at Jenna's forehead, calling her a total loser. "I'm going to go," said Susan into the screen, not sure if Jenna could hear.

"Wait," said Jenna, trying to shove Amber out of the shot. "No wait, I haven't even created, what was it called? Dissonance? I haven't created dissonance yet. Priggy and Champs were going on about smoking or something and how I have to—"

"You shouldn't be talking to the girls, especially if you want to do your school placement here."

Amber was shouting again in the background. "Is that all she ever does? Tells you what you can and can't do?"

"They won't be there in September," said Jenna, still trying to move Amber out of the shot. "They'll be at uni."

"Look, I'm going to go."

"No, wait."

Amber was back in the screen. "Sorry, Susie, it's Flaming Fridays down at Maimies and they've got a Sambuca special going on. Jade's meeting us there in an hour."

"No she's not," said Jenna into the screen.

"She is!" shouted Amber. "So are the men! Come on, girl, let's get ready. Sambuca, Sambuca, Sambuca."

"Have a good night," said Susan. "I'll speak to you soon."

****

Jenna watched the image of Susan drain away from her screen. "You are *such* a pain, Amber!"

"What?" said Amber, lifting up one of Jenna's scarfs from her cabinet and starting to dance. "Sambuca, Sambuca, Sambuca."

"You can't just come crashing into my room, announcing to my girlfriend that we're off to meet the lady who kissed me last night."

"But we are, and I can't wait to see what Paul plies me with tonight. He just kept that Champagne flowing." Amber nodded. "I really do think he could be the one."

"Well Susan's my one, and you've got to stop posting pictures of me."

"Stop giving me pictures to post!" Amber pulled a face. "Look at you, Jenna. You're sitting there with the word knobber stamped across your forehead looking utterly miserable. What's happened to you?"

Jenna reached for her make-up remover and squeezed some onto a piece of cotton wool. She started to rub. "I'm not happy."

"Thank goodness for that! You're finally being honest about the situation! So end it. End it all now."

"Okay, I will," said Jenna, pointing to the door. "Out you go."

"What?"

"I've had enough. I want you to leave. I want you to delete every picture you've ever posted of me, and I want you to leave."

"What? Why?"

"Because I'm leaving too."

CHAPTER TWENTY ONE

Jenna watched as her door slammed shut, really tempted to jump back up and apologise. She hated the idea that she had upset anyone, even if that person most probably deserved it. She stopped herself and thought about the priority at hand. An email to Susan. An email declaring her love. An email declaring her plans. An email that would create that dissonance and stop Susan from smoking. No, she thought, smiling to herself. Just an email. Just her words. Just the truth. Much better than a phone call where things could be misheard or misinterpreted. Just words. Words that would speak for themselves.

"Susan," she wrote. "My darling." No, she thought, deleting the second bit. "My love." No, she thought, deleting again and pressing enter. "I'm just going to write. I'm going to write and see what comes out. Then I'm going to send, without re-reading because I know if I re-read I'll cringe at myself and all of the clichés I'm probably about to use. So I'm sorry. But I love you. You're my one. My life. My world. You complete me. You make me want to be a better person. You've shown me the way, the truth, the light. Ahhhhh, no, I'm stopping. Okay, what is it I want to say?" Jenna paused for a moment. "I want to say that I want you. I need you. I need you in my life right now."

Jenna nodded at her progress and pressed enter, starting a new paragraph. "Susan, I'm a different person to the Jenna I was. I want different things. I want a different life. I want that because of you. You've changed me. In a good way. I'm done with all of the parties and stupid nights out. I'd much rather just snuggle up with you and stroke your hair." Jenna cringed as she wrote it. "It sounds ridiculous I know, but it's true. I just want to be with you. All of the time. I love being with you. There's this electric chemistry between us, and I know we both feel it. It's there every time we step into each other's space. It's magnetic and indescribable, and I never really believed anything like this existed. But it does, and I've found it with you. You're my match,

Susan, and we set off such a spark in each other." Jenna paused, feeling the goose bumps all over again.

"It's so easy to get sexual with you, but I won't. Not this time. This time I want to get emotional. I want you to feel me. Really feel what I feel, if that makes sense? My heart feels bigger. My soul feels fuller. My mind's just completely consumed by thoughts of you. I'm dreaming, Susan. I'm dreaming of the future. Our future. Our house. Our home. Our family. I'm sorry if that's too much for you, but that's where my mind goes. I can't stop it from wandering. It wanders and then it wonders. We have our whole lives ahead of us, Susan, and I'm so excited by our future. The places we'll visit. The people we'll meet. The friends we'll make together. We're a really good match. We complement each other. Even something silly like the way you fit perfectly under my arm when we're walking. Stuff like that shows me we're meant to be. You calm me down, Susan. You calm me down, and you help me see clearly. I see what I want. I want you. Here. Now. Forever." Jenna quickly pressed enter, feeling the words in full flow.

"It's like I finally understand what all the fuss is about. All of the people who talk about love with that glint in their eye. Well now I'm glinting and glowing, and I might even find myself gurning sometimes with glee." Jenna smiled to herself. "Susan, I'm shining so brightly that I light up every room every time your name is mentioned ... and your name gets mentioned a lot ... because I'm constantly bringing you up. I'm constantly pulling the conversation back around to you, or us, or our future. People are getting fed up with me, but I don't care. I want to talk about you. I want to tell the world how happy I am. How I've met the one. How everything's fallen into place just like a giant jigsaw that's been unsolvable for the whole of my life. Suddenly it's easy. Suddenly I know what the bigger picture looks like. Suddenly everything's slotting together and making such sense." Jenna paused. "My life's no longer a jumble of jagged pieces with me forcing things together only to find they don't fit. Suddenly my life's whole. My picture's whole. My puzzle's no more. My jigsaw's complete. All because of you."

Jenna nodded to herself. "I no longer have any questions. I understand everything. *Everything*, Susan. It's simple. I was made for you, and you were made for me, and our lives up to this point have just been our journeys to finding one another once more. We fit, Susan. We're one, and I know I said I wanted to be emotional not sexual, but I'm sorry, it has to be mentioned. We're explosive in bed. We're a match, quite literally, that's lit and ready to burn. In fact we're more like two sticks of dynamite. You're such a natural, with a hint of inner wickedness that drives me absolutely crazy. The look you get in your eye when you want me. I don't think you have any idea just how arousing you are, or just how satisfied you make me. I can't get enough of you. I won't *ever* be able to get enough of you. You're loud, you're confident, and you're crazier than I'd ever imagined was possible."

Jenna sighed. "But I miss you. If I'm honest I thought these three months would fly by. I love skiing. I love my job. Hey, I used to love my life. But now everything feels different. So…" Jenna paused. "Here comes the important bit. The bit I've thought long and hard about since I left you with two dildos shoved under your jumper - long and hard thinking, not long and hard dildos. I'm going to hand in my notice. I'm going to leave. I've been with Club Ski for five years now. I know how this works. They'll let me go. We've got the staff to cover my groups. There won't be an issue. I just know I need to be near to you. I won't crowd you though: I'll check in with my family, I'll check up on my flats, I'll call Sheila from Stage School and see if there are any slots available. I was thinking of starting a group for really little ones, maybe calling it *Dribbling Dramatics* or something like that, and focusing on facial expressions and noises. You know how new mums are. They'll sign their kids up for anything. But anyway, my point is, I'd be around. We could date. We could do all of the normal things that normal couples do."

Jenna paused for a moment and ran her fingers through her hair. "This is hard, isn't it? Harder than either of us ever thought it would be. The distance is too great, and social media's the scourge of society. Now do you understand why I hate Facebook and Instagram and all of those other sites? I've asked Amber to delete all of the pictures of me. I'll ask Hugo to do the same too. I know it's not appropriate to have those sorts of shots accessible on the internet. I want to conduct myself professionally. I want to teach. I want to teach alongside you."

"So," typed Jenna, wondering how she could make her point really clear, "I'm flying back. I want us. I want you. I want forever." She lifted her fingers from the keypad and brought them together in front of her mouth, smiling in her decision. She glanced down as a small ping sounded in the corner of her screen. It was an email alert. An email from Susan. She clicked on the link and started to read.

"Jenna," it said, "I'm just going to say this. We're not working." Jenna gasped, unable to stop her eyes from reading. "We both know the truth. It's over. In fact I'm not even sure it properly began. Please don't contact me for a while because I really need some space. I just don't want to feel like this anymore. Don't think this means you can't teach. You can. You'll be a brilliant teacher, and maybe, if you do get your placement over here, then we can start off again, as friends. But us? As a couple? We were never going to work." Jenna read the last line, simply signed: "Susan."

"No," gasped Jenna, dropping her head into her hands. She kept her eyes closed and tried to control her breathing, eventually finding the courage to peep through the fingers, hoping that the words would have changed. "No," she whispered once more, as her heart broke completely. Jenna dropped a hand and lifted a finger, feeling her stomach recoil in pain. She tapped on the mouse pad and clicked back to her own email. She scrolled to the send button and hovered over the pad, sighing slowly as she swiped the other way and clicked on delete instead.

CHAPTER TWENTY TWO

Susan walked down the wide stone steps in front of the school's main entrance, glimpsing the last glowing remains of the sunset across the acre, pleased to be out in the fresh air a lot earlier than anticipated. She turned around and watched Danielle Watts manoeuvre the red mobility scooter down the twisting access ramp. "We'll be quicker if we walk," shouted Susan.

Danielle pulled on the handlebar and turned the final corner. "I came this early on the condition we'd drive up. Hollyoaks hasn't even started yet." She tapped the wire basket at the front. "Plus this is perfect for my snacks. Shall I throw you a Malteser? We can pop Martha's port in here on the way back."

Susan shook her head and started to walk down the long drive that wound its way through the school grounds leading out towards the main road. "No thanks, I'll see you up there."

Danielle twisted the speed setting on the dashboard and pulled on the throttle. "No you won't!" she shouted, whizzing past Susan. "I'll see *you* up there!"

Susan started to jog. "Why's it going so fast?"

"Mary's tinkered with the settings. Come on! Jump on!" Danielle shouted over her shoulder. "Who's this friend we're meeting?"

Susan increased her pace. "She's called Felicity. She was in my year at school."

"Why's she out so early? It's not even half six."

Susan was running flat out. "She's just moved back into the Westbury Homes estate, asked if I'd like to catch up."

"This early on a Friday night?"

"No," shouted Susan, panting, "I just messaged her. I needed to get out. I couldn't wait until ten."

"Your Jenna Skype didn't go well then I take it?"

"What?" shouted Susan, falling too far behind.

Danielle pulled on the brakes, screeching to a stop. She reached into the basket and broke off a chunk of chocolate from her family-sized bar. "Your Skype with Jenna? It didn't go well?"

Susan slowed to a halt and dropped her hands onto her knees, catching her breath. "You were listening then? In the staffroom?"

"Hey, I'm the school nurse. It's my job to pay attention to the health and wellbeing of the residents and attendees here at St Wilfred's." She stuck the scooter in reverse and drew up alongside Susan. "Ears always open. Here, have some cola."

Susan refused the outstretched bottle and pulled herself upright. "Does that thing have a slow?"

"No, now hop on. There's room behind me."

Susan looked at the padded leather seat. "It's almost dark, I guess." She paused. "And it doesn't look like anyone's about."

"Exactly, we'll be up there in no time." Danielle revved the engine. "Just like Thelma and Louise."

Susan took a deep breath and threw her leg over the seat, tucking herself in behind Danielle. "Take it steady though."

"Of course," said Danielle, twisting the speed knob back up to high. "Health and wellbeing and all that. Hey, someone else I've been watching is Daisy. Little Daisy Button in Year Seven. You brought her to me with that rash."

Susan grabbed on to Danielle's waist as the scooter burst into life. "Y-y-yes. What about her?"

Danielle pulled even harder on the throttle. "Can albinos turn into oompa loompas?"

"W-w-what?" said Susan, feeling the wind in her hair.

"She's so tiny anyway, but now she's started to look orange. I mean it's more than an orange tint. It's oompa loompa orange. I was wondering if the two syndromes are connected."

"What?" said Susan, furiously trying to blink a fly out of her eye.

"Her pigmentation. It's changed from see-through white to glow-stick orange."

"There!" shouted Susan, squeezing Danielle's waist, thrilled at the opportunity to slow their speed. "That's her up ahead. Look, she's next to that patch of soil with Timmy and Bob. Let's slow down a bit, shall we? We can check on her."

"You can't be too obvious about these things," said Danielle, loosening her grip on the throttle. "Don't make her feel self-conscious."

"What's that up ahead?" said Susan.

"Where?"

"In the road."

Danielle was glancing from left to right. "I can't see anything."

"It looks like a spade, be careful!"

"Where?" Danielle started to slow the mobility scooter.

"Down there. Be careful!"

"Oh bugger," said Danielle as the front tyre hit the metal.

"It's a rake," shouted Susan as the long wooden stick shot up and hit Danielle on the side of the head, almost knocking her off her seat.

"Oww!" screamed Danielle, grabbing hold of the brake and trying to keep her balance. "My head!"

Susan clung on for dear life as the scooter slowed to a stop. "Are you okay?"

Danielle fell dramatically from the seat. "No I'm not okay! I've just been smacked in the face by a rake!"

"Ladies, are you okay? What's happened? What's happened I say?" Bob was struggling down the grassy mound with Daisy and Timmy in tow.

"Do I look okay to anyone?" shouted Danielle, nursing the red welt on the side of her head.

"Let me see," said Susan.

"Hi, Madam Quinn. Hi, Madam Watts." Daisy Button was smiling and waving a crutch.

Susan shook her head. "No, it's got too dark; I can't see properly."

Danielle looked up at the small group congregated around her. She caught sight of Daisy's orange face and gasped. "Daisy! You're glowing! We need some light. Come over here and shine on my forehead."

"I said she looks glowing too," said Timmy, smiling in Daisy's direction.

Daisy stepped up to her teacher and whispered. "St Tropez, brighter than bright. It was Margaret's idea. Hypoallergenic."

Susan smiled at the white eyes. "Timmy seems to like it."

"I know," she said with a giggle.

"Is anyone going to help me?" shouted Danielle. "I need some ice!"

"Shall I run back up to the school and get some?" asked Susan.

Bob shook his head. "The pub's closer."

"Can you make it to the Black Bear, Danielle?" asked Susan.

"No! Of course not! I'm injured." Danielle reached up to the scooter's basket. "I need a sugar rush. I'm feeling light headed."

"I'll be as quick as I can," said Susan.

"This is an emergency!" shouted Danielle. "Take the scooter!"

"I'm not taking the mobility scooter," said Susan.

"Take it! I NEED that ice!"

Susan jumped at the tone and mounted the scooter, twisting the speed dial half way and pulling on the throttle. "I'll be back in a bit."

"A glass of ice cold cola would help too," said Danielle, fanning her wound.

"Noted," said Susan, sticking her chin out and heading towards the school gates. She upped her speed slightly and tried not to smile at the thrill the ride was inducing. She turned the scooter left out of St Wilf's driveway and mounted the curb, heading around the short corner towards the Black Bear. She picked up her speed and drove straight towards the doors of the old English pub.

"Susan? Susan is that you?"

Susan slowed the red mobility scooter and looked towards the voice. Felicity Fenwick had just stepped out of her white Audi R8. "Felicity. Hi." Susan tried to switch off the power button but pipped the horn instead. "Sorry, I—"

"No, I'm sorry." Felicity dashed over, looking genuinely concerned. "I didn't realise you were disabled. I would have come and picked you up." She placed an arm around Susan's shoulder. "Come on, let's get you in out the cold."

****

"I can't believe you thought I was disabled," laughed Susan, taking a sip of her sparkling white wine.

"You arrived on a red mobility scooter. What was I meant to think?" Felicity smiled. "At least that Danielle drove herself back up to the school on it. What a drama queen. She'd have put a real dampener on the evening."

"No, Danielle's lovely. But thanks for your help. I don't think I could have managed the ice *and* the cola whilst steering that thing."

"Hey, I only wanted a ride. I might even see if they've got one on my company car list."

Susan laughed and sighed at the same time. "It's really good to get out."

"Missing Jenna?"

"Umm." Susan glanced around the interior of the old black and white timber building. There were a few regulars milling around the bar, and a loved-up couple at the table next to the jukebox, but it was still fairly early and the evening's musician hadn't even started to set up yet. She took a deep breath and found the courage to say the words. "Actually, we've decided to take a step back."

Felicity looked shocked. "Really? Why?"

"Oh I don't know. Because I'm an idiot."

"Did she end it?"

"No, I did."

"Was it mutual?"

Susan shrugged. "Probably. If I'm honest I think I've done her a favour. You were right. Just like everyone else was right. Long distance relationships don't work, especially if they're as young and fragile as ours is. Was."

"And Jenna's fine with this?"

"I don't know. I've asked for some space. I just hate the way I've been feeling. Always anxious about what she's been up to. Feeling like I'm holding her back with my neediness." Susan shook her head. "No, I'm right. I've done the right thing."

Felicity ran her finger around the rim of her wine glass. "So you're back on the market then?"

Susan coughed. "Well, no. I-I-I wouldn't quite say that."

"You're not single?"

"Well, yes. No. Well, I guess I am." Susan shook her head. "I'm not sure actually. I've asked for some space, but yes, it's far too early for me to start thinking about dating or anything." She laughed. "Well no, I've never even really dated before."

"Do you realise you're cute when you stumble on your words?"

"That's what Jenna says. Said."

Felicity moved a mound of flame-red hair to the other side of her head. "What else did Jenna say?"

"About what?"

"About you."

Susan felt her ears starts to flush. "Like what?"

"Oh you know. Does she tell you how much you've changed since school? How you've sort of done this Supergirl transformation, from someone you might not even have noticed, into someone you simply can't take your eyes off."

Susan tucked her hair behind her ears and looked down at the table, immediately moving her hands back up to re-adjust her hair and hide her ears that were now really quite red. "I haven't changed that much."

"You hooked Jenna James! Trust me you've changed."

"She *was* the school's resident hottie, wasn't she," said Susan with a smile.

"She sure was." Felicity angled her body towards Susan's. "You'd give her a run for her money now though."

Susan coughed again. "No, no. Tell me about you. I've been talking far too much."

Felicity was smiling. "The way you can't take a compliment. That's cute too." She paused. "Susan, are you uncomfortable with me chatting you up?"

"Don't be silly. You're not chatting me up."

"I might be."

Susan gulped a large mouthful of wine. "Shall I get us another?"

"Please," said Felicity, keeping her eyes on Susan.

Susan lifted her purse from the table and walked towards the bar, fully aware that Felicity would be staring if she turned back around. She slotted herself in front of a stool and jumped up, trying to look as casual as she could. What was happening? Why was Felicity flirting? What could she do? How could she handle it? Where would it lead? Susan paused her thought as she spotted Angel thanking her final customer and knew she had to focus. She would be over in a minute. It had to sound spontaneous. An off-the-cuff question. Nothing serious. No accusations. Just a quick comment that should evoke a response, and hopefully appease her concerns. Susan thought back to this afternoon's strange encounter once more, replaying what she thought she'd heard Angel say. Marcus couldn't possibly want her to dress up like a sch—

"Madam Quinn! That sounded so funny when my mister smoochy pants said it, didn't it, honey?" Angel was leaning over the bar. "I'll have to get used to calling you that if my Tammy and Tanisha start going."

Susan cleared her throat. "Do you think they will?"

"Oh yes, honey. My mister smoochy says anything's possible. It's just such a shame I didn't get to see the whole school. I had to get back up here for my shift, didn't I, honey. But he's promised me he'll show me his apartment in the staff living quarters next." She clicked a piece of chewing gum between her teeth. "So what can I get you?"

157

"Two glasses of sparkling white wine please." Susan watched as the barmaid reached up for the glasses. "Sorry, I tried to catch you earlier when you were leaving my room. You made me laugh actually. Was that a Britney Spears song I heard you singing?"

"What, honey?"

"In my classroom. To Marcus. I've just not heard it for a while. It always makes me smile."

Angel rolled her eyes. "Are all teachers like this?"

"Pardon?"

"You want me to sing it for you too, honey?"

"No, no."

Angel filled the second glass. "I'm teasing you. That's her best song. Dressed up like a school girl and all that."

"He's asked you to dress up like a school girl?"

Angel looked shocked. "I didn't just say that. Did I just say that? I'm not meant to say that. My mister smoochy pants is very particular about keeping things private."

"But he's asked you to do it?"

Angel handed over the drinks. "We're not at that stage yet, honey. I told you before; I want to take it slowly with this one. Too many broken hearts and all that." She winked. "But I love a bit of dress up, don't you?"

Susan frowned. "But he's a teacher."

"Fantasies are fantasies, that's all." Angel looked puzzled. "Honey, are you trying to say something?"

"No, no. Sorry. That song just made me smile." Susan handed over a ten pound note. "Thanks, Angel. Keep the change."

"He's a good guy is my mister smoochy."

Susan picked up the glasses. "Is he?"

Angel smiled knowingly. "Reminds me of you actually, honey. Very similar. Both slightly misunderstood."

"I don't think—"

"Sorry, sweetie pie, I've got a customer."

Susan watched as Angel tottered her way to the other side of the bar. *Similar?*

"Are you okay?" asked Felicity as Susan finally made her way back to the table. "You look a bit pained. Was that barmaid chatting you up as well?"

"Angel? No, no. I'm fine. It's fine." She put the drinks down and took her seat. "Well no, actually it's not fine. Can I ask you a quick question?"

"Sure."

"But don't read anything into it."

"Okay."

Susan settled herself down and tapped her teeth together. "Is it wrong for a teacher to want someone to dress up like a school girl?"

"Hit me baby one more time."

"Exactly."

"Everyone loves a bit of Britney."

"Do they?"

Felicity nodded. "If you asked me to dress up like a school girl then I'd do it."

"Really?"

"Yes, but I look much better in a sexy SWAT outfit."

"What if it was a male teacher asking someone to dress up like a school girl?"

Felicity pulled a face. "I'd think he was a filthy bastard."

Susan laughed. "Sorry, this isn't funny."

"What's not funny?"

Susan paused for a moment before shaking her head. "No, it's fine. Forget about it."

"I'm a good listener."

"So am I. Tell me about you. What have you been up to since our days at St Wilf's?"

Felicity smiled. "No, come on, talk to me."

Susan lifted her glass and shook her head. "No, you go; I'm thirsty."

"Okay then, well, I've calmed down, grown up, trained as a nurse, then a vet." She paused. "Gave up on both. I joined the police for a year, gave up on that. Now I'm selling pharmaceuticals for the UK's largest pharmaceutical company."

"And how's that going?" said Susan with a smile.

"It's good actually, but I think I might be getting a bit bored."

"You could always become a teacher."

"And get you to dress up as Britney?"

Susan blushed. "No, I meant—"

"You're so easy to tease!" Felicity was laughing. "I think I'll keep doing it because you're so cute when you blush."

Susan took another sip of wine. "Jenna calls me an animal in bed."

Felicity almost fell off her chair. "What! Where did that come from?"

"I'm not sure I like the label *cute*."

"Are you flirting with me, Susan Quinn?"

Susan caught hold of herself. "No, no no. Sorry no." She thought of Jenna and felt a pang of remorse. "No, sorry I wasn't."

"Well I'm flirting with you," said Felicity, leaning over and kissing Susan full on the lips.

CHAPTER TWENTY THREE

Susan stepped out of the shower, still feeling the pain of deep remorse. She hadn't asked Felicity to kiss her. She hadn't expected the come on. She hadn't encouraged the flirting. Susan paused as she flicked her head upside down and wrapped her hair in a towel. Or had she? Had she given off a vibe? Was she to blame? Her mind followed the same train of thought that it had taken last night. Is this what had happened to Jenna? Was Jenna really not at fault? Susan swallowed, still feeling physically sick. She had hardly slept a wink, and her late night attempts to call Jenna had ended with an automated message telling her that this person's phone was switched off. Susan picked up the second large towel and wrapped it around her body. She walked out of the bathroom and stepped up onto her bed, sitting down on the throw in the corner and drawing her knees up to her chest. She felt dirty. She felt guilty. Susan shook her towelled head at herself. She felt like she'd been unfaithful. Her message tone pinged and she reached out quickly, swiping her phone from the bedside table, but moaning in disappointment when Felicity's name flashed up. Susan read the message. It was the third one that morning, apologising once more for misreading the situation and hoping they'd still be able to continue their chat and catch up as friends, as it had all been going so well. Susan took a deep breath. It *had* been going so well, and Felicity *would* possibly make a really great friend. She'd be close. She'd certainly be exciting. Susan paused. But she'd tried to kiss her. Susan shook her head. Felicity wouldn't do it again though, especially not after her dramatic dashing from the pub and wailing that she wanted Jenna. She started to type: **I over-reacted. I'm sorry. I'd love to catch up again soon.**

Susan dropped the phone back down. Is this what Jenna had done? Ignored the misdemeanour and moved on? Amber was Jenna's colleague, Jade was Jenna's customer; of course she had to keep them close. Susan dropped her head into her hands, feeling like a total fool.

Someone *could* kiss you, and it didn't have to be your fault. Someone *could* cross the line, and you'd choose to keep them close. Susan bit her bottom lip and held back a tear. "*What have I done?*" she whispered into the silence, pulling her towel tighter around her body and sliding deeper into the bed, hoping it would swallow her whole. She lifted her head momentarily, thinking she'd heard a noise, but dropped it back down when she realised she hadn't. Life was so difficult, she thought. So hard to get right. Why wasn't there a manual? Why didn't— She lifted her head again, this time freeing an ear from her towel. Yes, there had definitely been a knock. A knock at the door. She pulled the towel back over her ear and sank her head into the pillow. There was nowhere she had to be. No one she had to meet. Whoever it was could just go away and take their issues elsewhere.

Susan heard the knocking again. She took a deep breath and rolled herself off the bed, checking she was still all tucked in. Maybe there was an emergency in the dorms, she thought, as she walked up to the door. Maybe Daisy Button was having an allergic reaction after plunging herself into a tar pit. She unlocked the latch and yanked on the handle. Maybe Champagne and Priggy—

"*Jenna?*" gasped Susan, as she pulled the door open.

"I'm sorry, I just—"

"JENNA!" shouted Susan, as she threw the door wide and grabbed hold of her girlfriend.

"Can I come—"

"JENNA!" screamed Susan, as she squeezed her in close and clung on for dear life.

Jenna managed to swing her holdall from the penguin position she'd been forced into, dropping it inside Susan's apartment. "I really am—"

"Stop," said Susan, smothering Jenna's neck, face and lips with kisses. "It's me, I—" Susan found herself unable to talk as Jenna's hands clutched her back and her lips met her mouth, Jenna's tongue pushing harder against her own. Susan staggered backwards, pulling Jenna into the apartment. She slammed the door shut and changed her direction, driving Jenna backwards against the door. The contact between them was hard and searing, and both knew they couldn't stop the moment even if they tried. Susan grabbed Jenna's neck, tilting her head upwards, forcing her own tongue deeper into her girlfriend's mouth. "Need you," she murmured, unable to control herself, thrusting her other hand up Jenna's top and squeezing her breast.

Jenna ripped the towel from Susan's body and pulled on the bare buttocks, drawing Susan in even closer. "Feel the energy," she whispered, in between the rough urgent kisses.

"It's more than energy," gasped Susan, removing her hand from Jenna's neck and plunging it down the front of her jeans, immediately tilting her fingers upwards and forcing herself inside. "You're so wet," she cried.

Jenna screamed out in pleasure. "Yes! Take me deeper."

Susan yanked her hand out of Jenna's jumper and thrust it against her mouth, silencing her screams. "You have to be quiet."

"I can't," cried Jenna between the fingers, as Susan pushed even deeper.

Susan tightened her grip over Jenna's mouth and pressed her body against her girlfriend's, slamming her naked breasts into Jenna's chest and using her thigh to thrust her fingers further inside. "Take more for me," gasped Susan, watching her girlfriend's eyes widen as she readjusted her hand.

Jenna cried out through the clasped fingers. Her voice was muffled. "I'm going to come!"

Susan quickened her pace, losing herself between her girlfriend's legs. "Now, Jenna," she urged, using her free thumb to jab upwards against Jenna's clit.

Jenna screamed, almost biting the hand that was pinning her by the mouth against the door. "Yes!" she cried. "Yes, yes, yes!"

Susan's final thrust almost lifted Jenna off the floor. "Fuck," she gasped to herself, flicking her head violently to the side and getting rid of the towel that had come loose. She kept her fingers in position and removed her hand from Jenna's mouth, holding Jenna by the cheek and kissing her passionately on the lips. She kept their chests together and felt both their hearts pounding at a crazy pace. She moved her lips to her girlfriend's ear and whispered. "It's more than energy, Jenna. We're connected. We're meant to be together. It's like a unique intensity that ignites when we're one."

Jenna slowly opened her eyes and whispered right back. "We're certainly connected right now."

"Sorry. You ready?" asked Susan.

Jenna kept her breaths shallow, moaning slightly as Susan removed her fingers. "Mmm, you're incredible."

"No," said Susan, shaking her damp hair around her shoulders, "I was rushed. I couldn't help it. But I'm going to make up for it now."

She kissed Jenna gently on the lips before taking her hand and guiding her around the corner towards the bed.

"You have the sexiest arse," said Jenna, watching the nakedness in front of her.

"It's yours. All of me belongs to you."

"To do what I want with?"

Susan stopped at the bed and turned around. "Yes, to do what you want with. But first I want to do you." She smiled and ran her thumb along Jenna's lips. "Slowly. Softly. With love." She took hold of the side of Jenna's jumper and lifted it off. "I think you just felt my passion." She unhooked the bra and let it drop to the floor. "Now I want you to feel my affection." Susan moved her slow kisses down Jenna's collarbone and over her breasts, letting her eyelashes flicker over Jenna's nipples. She pushed on the sides of Jenna's jeans and wiggled them past her bottom. "Sit down on the bed," she said, dropping onto her own knees on the carpet. She pulled at the jeans, pants, and socks, and looked up at her girlfriend, naked, with just her tousled brown hair cascading around her shoulders. Susan stared into Jenna's big eyes and shook her head. "I love you so much, and I'm so, so, sorry."

Jenna reached out and took Susan's face in her hands. "I'm sorry too. I love you, Susan. Make love to me. Please, make love to me."

Susan lifted herself up on her knees and kissed the woman who meant more to her than anyone had ever done before. "I know we need to talk, but not yet. Let's just savour the moment." She smiled. "You're here. I'm here." She pulled Jenna's bottom further towards the edge of the bed, causing Jenna to wrap her legs around her back. "You're wet. Why talk?"

"No need," said Jenna, pulling Susan in for a long, slow embrace. "Come up here on the bed with me."

"Not yet," said Susan, kneeling back down. "Wrap your legs around my shoulders. I want to kiss you."

"You've been kissing me."

"I want to kiss you properly," said Susan, causing a moan of anticipation in Jenna, who did as instructed and wrapped her legs around Susan's shoulders, crossing them at the ankles.

"I'm just going to kiss you," said Susan once more, "kiss you like I love you."

Jenna leaned back on her arms, letting her head drop backwards, stretching her neck up towards Susan's ceiling. She moaned lightly as her body was drawn further forwards, her legs parted with Susan's mouth. "I need to touch you too," she gasped. "I need—" she cried out as Susan's tongue pushed inside her. "Keep going," she said instead. "Yes, yes, keep going."

Susan held tightly onto the back of Jenna's body, her palms flat against the skin, pulling her closer, burying her head deeper. She kissed Jenna's warmth like she would her mouth, moaning into her lips and pressing passionately into her opening. Jenna tasted so good. So soft. So inviting. Susan kissed harder, overcome with desire, pressing her nails into Jenna's back and forcing her tongue deeper.

Jenna took her weight on one hand and used the other to grab the back of Susan's head, keeping her in position and adding more pressure. "Fuck me, Susan. Just fuck me!"

Susan swallowed more of Jenna, flicking her tongue faster and adding a rotating motion with her head. She pulled on Jenna's buttocks, parting her with both hands from behind. Her fingers sliding into Jenna's warmth, allowing her mouth time to focus on her clit. She encased it fully and pushed her tongue flat against it, moving in slow hard circles.

Jenna was gasping at the assault from all angles, crying out that she was really close. "More!" she shouted.

Susan pulled outwards with each finger that was inside, opening Jenna further, preparing her for more. She added another finger from each side, filling Jenna completely, increasing the pressure with her tongue.

Jenna was tilting her pelvis upwards, almost taking charge of the pace against Susan's mouth, still holding on to the back of Susan's head. "I'm coming," she screamed, fucking herself forwards one final time.

Susan stayed in position, feeling Jenna tighten around her fingers and quiver against her tongue, aware of the rush of moisture against her chin. She held her position before calming her breathing and pulling away, using the bottom of the bedspread to discreetly pat her face. She knelt back up and gasped. "Sorry, I somehow ended up fucking you again. I just haven't got the control to take my time with you."

Jenna let her arm buckle underneath her and flopped backwards onto the bed. "This trip has already been worth my while."

"How long are you—" Susan stopped herself. "No, not yet. No talking. Let's just lie together. Can I just hold you?" She climbed up onto the bed, relieved to stretch out her knees. "Come on," she said, pulling back the covers. "Come tuck yourself under here with me."

Jenna shuffled herself up the bed and under the warm duvet. "Can I try?" she said.

Susan moved some of the long brown waves behind Jenna's ear. "Try what?"

"Try and make love to you." She smiled. "I don't think half of my body's working any more so it's not like I'm going to fling you into the seesaw or the rodeo."

Susan laughed. "Have we done those yet?"

"Probably," said Jenna, slowly rolling on top of Susan's body and parting her legs with her own. "But I'll only be capable of making limited movements for the next five minutes or so." She rested herself on her elbows either side of Susan's arms. "Like maybe this one," she said, slowly moving her thigh against Susan's warmth.

Susan moaned. "That one's good."

"Or this one," whispered Jenna, gently pressing her breasts into Susan's and circling their nipples together.

"Mmm, that one's good too."

Jenna dropped her head, moving her lips onto Susan's in such an exquisitely gentle fashion that it almost made Susan cry. Susan returned the tender embrace, pulling back slightly and losing herself in Jenna's emotion-filled eyes, uttering the words that came so easily. "I love you so much."

"I know," said Jenna, gently building up a slow rhythm with her hips. "I'm here *because* I know."

Susan lifted her hands to Jenna's cheeks, rubbing them lightly with her thumbs. "I forgot, didn't I? You told me not to forget, but I did." She closed her eyes and rested her head on the pillow. "How could I forget? How could I possibly forget this?"

Jenna kissed the tops of Susan's eyelids. "You didn't forget, you just needed reminding."

"Mmm," moaned Susan as Jenna pushed more deeply with her thigh. "Isn't that the same thing?"

"No, gorgeous, just relax. Just feel me."

Susan opened her eyes and stared into Jenna's soul. "I feel you everywhere. With every single beat of my heart. With every single thought in my head." She smiled. "With every single tingling hair on my body." She gasped as Jenna gently circled her nipple with her tongue. "My nerve endings feel you. Every single one of them."

"Good," said Jenna, silencing Susan with her lips, "because I love you."

Susan gasped as Jenna kissed deeper, moving their bodies as one, arousing her slowly, fully, perfectly.

Making love.

CHAPTER TWENTY FOUR

Susan lifted her legs onto Jenna's and reached down for her cup of tea. Both were now dressed after their morning in bed and sitting on the sofa, neither really looking forward to the chat they were about to have, but realising they had to have it all the same.

"Shall I start?" asked Jenna.

Susan took a nervous sip of tea and nodded. "Okay."

"I emailed you yesterday, after our Skype, after Amber barged in."

"I didn't get it," said Susan with a frown.

Jenna shrugged. "I deleted it. I was about to press send when yours came through."

"Did your email say the same thing as my email?"

"God no!" gasped Jenna. "I was pouring my heart out. I was declaring my love! I think I almost popped a marriage proposal in there at one point."

"No."

"I might as well have done." She took Susan's mug of tea and placed it back down on the floor, reaching up to hold Susan's hands. "I'm head over heels in love with you, Susan. I wanted to make things right. I wanted you to understand the bigger picture." She shook her head. "I didn't kiss Jade, and I hadn't planned on meeting her again last night, no matter what Amber said. The thought of you hurt by the whole fiasco was killing me. I had to email you. I had to connect with you. I had to get you to feel me. I had to get you to understand. I'm in this, Susan. I'm in this forever."

"I'm so sorry."

Jenna smiled. "There's no need. Everything's fine now, but amongst all of my clichéd ramblings was my news."

"No, I'm sorry."

"Forget it. Let me tell you my news."

Susan looked away. "I kissed someone."

"My exciting news about ..." Jenna paused. "What? When?" She bent her head and tried to catch Susan's eyes. "Who?"

Susan didn't look up. "Felicity Fenwick."

"In school?" Jenna laughed. "Ha! I always knew you were gay. So what? What does that matter? Are you going to confess to having had a slew of lesbian lovers?" She smiled. "I don't care. At least it explains why you're so good in bed."

"Last night."

Jenna paused. "What?"

"Last night. I kissed Felicity Fenwick, last night. Well, no, she kissed me. But maybe I was to blame. I did agree to go for drinks with her after all, and maybe I gave off signals." Susan's eyes were back and pleading. "But I didn't mean to. She came on to me. Our lips met, and maybe to someone watching it might have looked like we kissed, but it was one-sided, and I ran off, and now I feel so guilty for judging you."

Jenna was frowning. "Why were you and Felicity Fenwick together last night?" She paused. "Oh no, Susan. Did you really mean what you wrote in your email? Did you end it because of her? Have I just made a total fool out of myself by flying back over here?"

"No! No! Of course not. She got back in contact. I got roped into going to the Black Bear by Martha and Mary, so I suggested we met. Danielle was meant to be coming out too but she got hit in the face by a rake and fell off the mobility scooter—"

"What?"

"Oh it doesn't matter. The point is, I understand." She picked Jenna's hand back up. "I trust you. I trust what you said about Jade. I trust that it wasn't your fault. I understand how it can happen."

"What was her name at school? Fuck-Em-All Felicity? She's a predator. I don't think you should see her again."

"She's harmless."

Jenna lifted her eyes, realising that Susan had clocked it too. "Is this how you felt when I called Amber harmless? When I called Jade harmless?"

"But Felicity *is* harmless."

"She kissed you! Do you like her?"

"Yes, as a friend. She's fun. She's in the area. I think she'll be good for me."

"Someone who tries to kiss you isn't good for you."

"Amber's constantly trying to kiss you!"

"No she's not!"

"Yes she is!" Susan shook her head. "Felicity's fine."

"Fine then."

"Good. I'm glad you trust me."

"I do, but I don't trust her. But anyway. My news. Right, here goes." Jenna paused. "Wait. You're sure you don't like her? You're sure there wasn't any chemistry?"

Susan laughed. "Okay I get it. I was an idiot bombarding you with my insecurities."

"No I'm serious. I need to know."

"Stop it," laughed Susan, shoving Jenna by the arm. "You've made your point."

"Stop what?" asked Jenna, confused.

"Tell me your news."

Jenna looked at Susan and tilted her head. "Is there something you're not telling me?"

"No! You're the one not telling me *your* news." She sighed. "I get it though. I've been a total loser. I forgot what we had. I forgot the strength of our connection. I forgot what I already knew." She nodded. "I already knew we were for keeps. I shouldn't have questioned anything."

Jenna smiled. "Really? You think we've got the happy ever after?"

"I know we have, and I know you know that too."

Jenna laughed. "Wow. One quick flight and a morning of sex can work wonders."

Susan squeezed Jenna's hands before reaching down for their mugs. "Here—"

"No, put them back down. I don't want you scalding yourself when you hear my news."

Susan laughed and put them back on the carpet. "You're pregnant."

"Yes, triplets. I'm also back. For good."

Susan gasped. "What? No. You're not?" She shook her head. "No, of course you're not. You've got to work. You've got to finish the season."

"I can get cover. Lisa's gone to pick up my school today, and there'll be someone available to take them this week."

"No," Susan was shaking her head. "No, you can't. It's your job. You love your job."

"I love you more."

Susan leaned forwards and wrapped her arms around Jenna's shoulders. "The thought's lovely. The fact you flew over here last night is lovely." She paused. "Hey, is that why I couldn't get through to you on your phone? Anyway, last night, or this morning, or whenever you did—"

"I left the moment I got your email."

Susan shook her head at herself. "I'm so sorry. I'm so ashamed of myself. But the fact you flew over to make things right has taught me the biggest lesson in love. If you feel it, it's real, and you should never let anyone tell you it isn't." She sighed. "I should have ignored the photos, the comments, the silly insecurities that I let creep in. I should have known."

"We're both new to this," said Jenna. "There were bound to be some teething problems."

"I think we've gone through three sets of dentures already." She shook her head at herself once more. "Please forgive me. I've been such a fool. Crikey, you're contemplating leaving your job because of my neediness."

"No, I'm leaving my job because I miss you. I want us. I want us right now."

"We have us already. We'll call, Skype and message. We'll get through this, Jenna. But you can't leave. You can't just jump ship. It wouldn't look good on your School Direct interview, and I know you, you love Club Ski. You'd hate to let them down."

"I said I'd call them this afternoon." She shrugged. "I didn't know if you were going to turn me away at the door, or how this might go. But they can cover it. I know they can."

"Lessons start tomorrow, don't they?"

"Yes, why?"

"We'll have lunch and I'll drive you back to the airport. There are dozens of flights out of London to Geneva on a Saturday. You'll be back in time to have the evening meal with your school and sort the staff out for the week ahead."

"No."

"Yes."

Jenna sighed. "I'm not happy over there."

"Because I was being a lunatic."

"No." She paused. "Well maybe a little bit. But I want to be with you. I want to have this every day."

"We will. Just not yet." Susan smiled. "Plus I think your pussy would be in plaster if we had this every day."

"Susan Quinn!" laughed Jenna.

"It would, but seriously I'm so touched at the thought, and you jumping on an impromptu flight to declare your love will take some beating in the romance stakes."

"I don't think I declared anything. I think you had your fingers inside me before I even stepped through the door. I actually only came back to collect some socks."

Susan batted her on the shoulder. "Stop it, and drink your tea, lady. We're on a mission to get you back to the airport."

"Do we have to?"

"Yes, we do."

****

"Why's the car park so busy?" asked Jenna as they stepped down onto the gravel path, having walked the long way round the red-brick building, desperate to prolong their departure as much as they could.

"Today's the first round of vice principal interviews."

"On a Saturday? Poor Battle-Axe Brown. The end of an era."

Susan nodded and glanced at the pale blue Clio that was potentially blocking her in. "Yes, I think it's a three part interview. Today's the tour of the school, and get to know you chats. The candidates will get a feel for St Wilf's and withdraw if it's not quite for them." Susan walked to the back of her car, judging the space between her and the Clio. "It just means there's not that awful situation when someone gets offered the job, only to turn it down minutes later."

"You think I'll have get to know you chats?"

Susan smiled. "No one else has applied for the School Direct Programme, so if you're called for interview it means they want you. The *whole thing* will be one big get to know you chat." She walked to the other side of the car. "The school has to subscribe to some form of teacher training each year, and this programme means they get their lessons covered without having to pay you."

"They'll use me?"

Susan stepped backwards, frowning at the jam. "No, you use them to get your NQT status. The Government pays for the programme." She shook her head. "I'm really not sure I can get out of here. Shall we just go back in for one more cup of tea? Flights are going out all afternoon."

"We've had five cups already! No, come on, we can't delay this any longer. Pass me the keys: I'll get us out."

"It's a Prius. You're sure?" Susan turned around as she heard the crunch of car tyres and the beeping of a horn.

"Mon amie, mon amie!" Marcus was leaning out of the window of his Fiat Punto Sport. "Are you leaving? Can I take your space? I'm continuing Angel's tour of the school today." Angel leaned across his lap and waved, causing Marcus to over rev the engine.

Jenna stepped into view and smiled. "Marcus! Great to see you again! So sorry to hear about your tribunal."

Marcus elbowed Angel back into her own seat. "What are you doing back?"

"Oh, just a romantic surprise visit. I had a spare morning so I thought I'd make the most of it with my gorgeous girlfriend."

Marcus sniffed. "Well you've got some competition coming your way. I've seen the candidates for the vice principal post." He let out a long, low whistle. "There's this one tall blonde lady with the most amazing blue eyes. She's surely the front runner. Shame you won't be around next year to keep an eye on Susan."

Susan butted in. "Jenna will hear about her School Direct interview any day now. They're bound to accept her."

Marcus scoffed. "Not if the tequila tit shots on Facebook are anything to go by."

Jenna took the keys from Susan and unlocked the car. "Watch yourself, Marcus. I wouldn't want to dent your trike."

"My what?"

"Sorry, I thought you peddled that thing. Come on, Susan, jump in." Jenna took a seat and slammed the door, staring at the confusing dashboard and wondering where on earth the ignition was.

Susan joined her in the passenger seat and fanned her face. "He's seen the photos! I bet he's made copies!"

"No, he'd have used them by now."

"How?"

"To try and get you to change your mind about his tribunal." She shook her head. "Amber says she's taken them off. He probably saw them ages ago."

Susan reached over and pressed the round power button. "And Hugo?"

Jenna tapped her foot against the floor wondering where the clutch was. "I'll give him a call when I get to the airport. But don't worry, the internet will be Jenna James free." She nodded as Susan pressed the reverse button. "Come on, let's churn up some gravel and try and chip him as we pass."

"Watch that car!" shouted Susan as Jenna swung around too quickly, narrowly missing the pale blue paintwork.

"It's fine, we're clear, let's go," said Jenna, slamming her foot to the floor, slightly disappointed when the Prius rolled silently out of the car park. "Bugger, I wanted to make a real exit. He's such a knob, and what the hell's that lady from the Black Bear doing with him? I thought she was nice."

Susan shrugged. "I think she likes him. They seem to be a genuine couple."

"Bollocks," said Jenna, hoping the car would pick up speed. "He's playing the *look I'm a taken man* card."

"The what?"

"You know. He's an upstanding professional with a loyal partner. No shenanigans here, governor."

"You think?"

"Yes, it looks better than him being a single male predator."

Susan laughed. "He's just a bit misguided."

"You still don't think he's done anything wrong, do you?"

"Oh I don't know. Can we stop talking about him? It's only half an hour to the airport. Let's talk about love instead."

Jenna smiled and tapped the indicator, rolling smoothly out of St Wilfred's long drive. "When you know, you know. And this time I know we'll be fine."

"Just fine," said Susan with a smile.

CHAPTER TWENTY FIVE

"No, I'm not fine!" wailed Susan, double crossing her legs.

"Just calm down," said Jenna, dropping her hand from the steering wheel and stroking Susan's thigh.

"Don't touch me! It'll come out!"

Jenna tried not to laugh. "The traffic's bound to move in a minute."

"You said that ten minutes ago!" Susan was jiggling in the passenger seat. "We shouldn't have had all those cups of tea!"

"Hey, you were the one who kept putting the kettle back on."

"Yes, because I wanted to delay your trip to the airport, but now I can't wait to see that bloody airport!"

Jenna checked the clock on the dashboard. "I think I'll have to catch the later flight. Nothing seems to be moving."

"You said we'd be moving in a minute!"

Jenna frowned. "Why does this car keep switching itself off?"

"It's a Prius! I need a wee and I seriously can't hold it any longer!"

"You have to," said Jenna, trying not to smile. "I'm surprised the *Prius* doesn't have an en-suite."

"I can't! And stop saying it like that!"

"We're on the M25. We're boxed in."

"So get me onto the hard shoulder. I'll climb the embankment. There are bound to be some trees."

"I can't. Nothing's moving."

Susan unbuckled her seat belt and started to bounce. "Maybe I could just nip out now?"

"You can't run across the carriageway!"

"So find me something to wee in! I'll get in the back seat. I seriously can't hold it."

Jenna glanced around the car, spotting the can of de-icer in the side of her door. She pulled it out and took off the lid. "This?" she said with a frown.

Susan triple crossed her legs and rocked from side to side. "Stop it! This is serious. I'm going to get a hernia."

"You're going to roll this tin can car if you keep that up."

"It's a Prius!"

Jenna shrugged. "It's stopped."

"It's energy saving!"

"Why don't you save some energy and just sit still?"

Susan upped her shaking. "Jiggling helps."

"You're swishing around ten pints of tea. Just relax and let your body absorb it."

"Jenna!" Susan's octave was high. "I can't! It's coming! It's seriously coming!"

"What's that blanket?" asked Jenna, turning around and pointing to the parcel shelf of the car.

"It's my Grandma's. She leant it me for picnics and stuff."

"So roll it up and piss on it. It's bound to be absorbent."

"Jenna!" Susan was snorting back the giggles. "You're making this worse! Seriously it's coming. It's coming any minute now."

Jenna reached into the back of the car and lifted up the small umbrella. "Open this up and wee in here. It's waterproof."

"The prongs will poke me. Plus it's bad luck."

"Just straddle it, Susan."

"Stop it! There must be something!"

Jenna pointed to the wing mirrors. "Look, there's a big lorry behind us and a big truck on your left hand side. Just open your door slightly and pop your bottom out."

"Will I get in trouble?"

"No, just keep your legs inside. It's not like you're stepping onto the fast lane." She tapped her own thighs. "Here, put your legs on me and just edge yourself backwards. I'll keep hold of your ankles."

Susan was wiggling, frantically surveying the situation. "What will I hold on to?"

"Hold the back of the head rest with one hand and the door handle with the other."

"Wait! I've got a torch in the glove box. I could take the batteries out and wee in there." She hit the mottled plastic and fished out the small flashlight, quickly unscrewing the bulb.

"You'll electrocute yourself, Susan! Plus it's only going to take two pipettes worth of piss."

"Jenna! It's coming!" screamed Susan, throwing the torch back down. "I'm sticking my bottom out! Take hold of my legs!" Susan pulled her jeans and pants down to her ankles and clung onto the head rest, opening the door slightly and edging her bottom out into the cold. "Am I far enough?" she shouted, catching her breath in the breeze.

Jenna glanced to the left before noticing the gap that had appeared ahead of them and the flashing of lights in her rear view mirror. "Hang on, Susan."

"What? Wait! No!"

Jenna heard the horn from behind and touched on the accelerator, bringing the car back to life. "Sorry," she gasped as the car shunted forwards.

Susan's arm pulled taut as her door flew open. She yanked on the head rest trying desperately hard to keep her bottom up. "You're dragging my arse along the M25! Stop the car would you?"

"I can't! We're moving!"

"I'm going to graze! Get me back in!"

"Have you done it yet?" shouted Jenna, continuing to roll forwards.

"No! I'm trying to stop myself from scuffing!"

"I'm going slowly. Just let it all out!"

"I can't!" cried Susan, hauling herself back into the car. She slammed the door shut and took a sharp breath. "It's coming! It's seriously coming!"

"Grab the blanket then!"

"No! It's mohair!" Susan frantically pulled on all the compartments close to her, yelping in glee as a small, yellow square dropped out of the dashboard bin.

"What? What is it?"

Susan wildly un-scrunched the yellow square. "It's a Quavers packet! I ate them yesterday!"

"And what are you going to do with that?" asked Jenna, trying to keep her eyes on the road.

"Straddle it!" screamed Susan, uncontrollably falling into the back of the car and pulling her jeans off at the ankle. She squatted in the foot well and fanned out the packet.

"Was it family-sized?" asked Jenna.

"What? No—" shouted Susan, adjusting her position and daring to unclench. She shuddered in orgasmic relief. "Ahh, it's coming."

"You're pissing into a packet of Quavers?"

"Yes, and it's beautiful. Wait, no, it's going too high!" Susan was recklessly throwing her head down between her legs, then back up again in a look of panic. "It's going to go over! It's going to go over!"

"Stop yourself!" shouted Jenna. "Squeeze!"

Susan squeezed the packet by mistake splashing warmth all over her fingers. "No!" she gasped as the flow continued. "I can't stop!"

Jenna glanced down into the foot well. "Bloody hell! It's like Niagara Falls back there!"

"It's not funny," cried Susan, sloshing the packet between her legs. "I'm still going!"

Jenna sniffed. "Cheese Quavers, or stinky piss?"

"It's the crisps! There were crumbs left in the packet." She glanced down. "Dissolved now though."

Jenna pulled a face. "Vaporised more like!"

Susan slowed her breathing and closed her eyes in relief. "Ahh, I think I'm done. Oh, no, wait, just a little bit more." She sighed again. "Yes, that's it. I'm done."

"Well thank heavens for that," said Jenna.

Susan stayed squatted as she glanced at the floor. "I think I might have got a little bit on the carpet."

"A little bit? That'll soak through. People will think we've got an oil leak."

"You have been zero help," said Susan, wiggling her bottom and shaking off the last of the drips. She sat backwards onto the seat and balanced the crisp packet in her palm. "Let me just tip this out of the window," she said, lifting the yellow bag, which was full to the brim. She held it in position and pressed the open button, shrieking out in horror as a gust of wind blew the bag backwards. "No!" she cried as it sloshed all over her shirt.

Jenna tried to swallow her laughter. "Look, we're really moving now. This is our junction."

"You swerved!" shouted Susan.

"I did not! You really think I want to stand in front of that check-in lady with you smelling of cat piss!"

"It's my piss!"

"She'll think we've progressed onto golden showers."

Susan tipped out the couple of remaining drips that were left in the bottom of the bag. "Oh good god," she said, looking down at the state of herself. "I'm so, so sorry."

Jenna shrugged. "It happens."

"Does it?"

"To you, Susan Quinn, yes it does." She looked in the rear view mirror and nodded. "Watch out though. That shirt's going to stain."

CHAPTER TWENTY SIX

Susan glanced down at her favourite white shirt, pleased that after three weeks the slight yellow tinge had finally come out. She picked a stray hair from the cuff and turned her attention back to her laptop and the latest romantic email from Jenna. She blushed and looked once more around the quiet school library. It was 6.00 p.m. and most of the day girls had gone home. The odd stray boarder continued to come out of the shelves, most probably making their way to the dinner hall, but for the most part Susan was alone. She smiled to herself, reading all about Jenna's latest school group, and swooning at her comment that there hadn't been a teacher as beautiful as her since their trip back in February. Susan clicked on the reply button and started to type.

Everything had been perfect since Jenna's impromptu flight over. It was as if they had started from scratch. The way it was meant to be in the beginning, without all the questions and insecurities. Just safe in the knowledge that they were in love, and both felt it completely. Susan tapped away, enjoying the freedom of that Friday night feeling. She'd been in the library since 3.00 p.m. marking books and planning lessons, and was now up to date and raring to go. She was meeting Felicity in the Black Bear at 8.00 p.m., along with a couple of Felicity's friends, who had started to become her friends too, so she knew she had plenty of time to tap away to her heart's content.

"So," wrote Susan, "I thought I'd make a list of all of the ways you make me happy…and yes, I am trying to 'out-cheese' the list you sent me of my top twenty most beautiful body parts. So, here goes:

You make me happy:
1. Every time you look at me.
2. Every time you smile.
3. Every time you finish your calls with *I love you.*
4. Every time you call me 'gorgeous.'

5. Every time you send me an actual letter in the actual post.

6. Every time you ask about my day.

7. Every time you send me a selfie.

8. Every time you sing me love songs and add my name to the lyrics.

9. Every time you—"

"Ahem, mon amie, I was wondering if I'd be able to borrow your laptop for un momento." Marcus was standing in front of Susan's work station, fumbling with something in the breast pocket of his well-worn tweed jacket.

Susan looked up from the screen and frowned. "You've asked me the same question at least three times over the last three weeks, and every time I've been busy. I'm sorry, Marcus, but you really should get your own sorted out."

"Fat Shirley from IT's leaving and she's slacking in her final few weeks."

"Marcus, it's her thyroid."

Marcus preened the corner of his moustache with his tongue. "Well good riddance to her *and* her doughnut addiction, and anyway, her replacement's almost sorted. Did you see the candidates today? There was this one red head who looked like she'd be ferocious in bed."

"Marcus!"

"Fight fire with fire, that's what they say." He ran his fingers through his thinning orange hair. "We'd be a perfect match, and I'm sure my Angel wouldn't be averse to a little ménage a trois."

"I don't want to know."

"I'm just bantering like I do with the boys. You're one of us now, aren't you? I'm embracing your love of the ladies." He stepped in closer and whispered. "Maybe we could share stories one day? Ooo, that reminds me. It was the second round of the history interviews as well and there was this one cute filly with a really naughty twinkle in her eye. Chestnut brown hair. Figure you'd fuc—"

"For goodness sake, Marcus. Just stop it." Susan returned her fingers to her keyboard.

"Let me quickly surf your nettage and I'll be on my way."

Susan nodded her head sideways. "Just use the library ones."

"But I'll have to log on, and the boot up takes ages."

Susan pressed the enter key with far more force than was required. She took a deep breath and looked up at Marcus. He was still fumbling with his jacket and appeared to be shifting his weight from foot to foot. "I'm really sorry, but I'm busy. You could have booted up ages ago."

"Mon amie, I've been making amends. I hope you've noticed my recent acts of gallant chivalry and—"

"Marcus, please."

He stayed silent for a moment before softening his voice. "I *had* been hoping you'd reconsidered my request as a character witne—"

"I'm sorry, I haven't. I'll be at the tribunal answering all of the questions as honestly as I can."

"Pfft, why does every one insist on calling it a tribunal? It's a silly little get together between a bunch of old fuddy duddys one night next week. The fact they haven't even confirmed the day yet should speak volumes." He straightened his neck. "Susan, she's setting me up."

"So shine on through. If you've done nothing wrong then you've got nothing to worry about. Why the desperation?"

Marcus narrowed his eyes. "This is *her* talking, not you. She's such a bad influence on you what with her feminist—"

"Daisy!" said Susan, thrilled to see the little girl hobbling past one of the wooden ladders.

"Shhhh!" snapped Marcus. "This is a library."

Susan ignored the scolding and signalled the little girl over. She pointed at the small black tablet tucked safely under Daisy's arm pit. "Is this it? The new gadget you were telling me about? What is it? An iPad, or a kindle fire?"

Daisy joined them at the workstation and leaned her crutches against the table, proudly pulling the electronic device from under her arm. "No, it's a Nipper. My mum says it's an exclusive."

Marcus took the black tablet from the little girl's hands and peered down at it. "Yes, exclusive to Tesco. I've seen these on offer next to the fruit and veg."

"Please be careful, Professor, it's taken us months to save up."

Marcus sniffed. "No 3G?"

"It's got a USB port. My mum says the iPads don't even have a USB port."

"It looks lovely, Daisy," said Susan. "Why don't you take a seat and talk me through it?"

Marcus continued to tilt the tablet and look at it in disgust. "Won't last more than a week. Real low end."

Daisy smiled. "Well I like it, and my mum even cried a little bit when she watched me unwrap it. It's the best present I've ever had. Could I have it back please, Professor?"

Marcus handed it over and wiped his fingers on his jacket. "Why are you still here? You're a day girl. It's Friday night."

Daisy smiled. "I've uploaded all of Bob's display designs for the flower patches. I'm going down to the gardens now. Me and Timmy are in charge. You can come too if you want, Madam Quinn. I can show you all of the stuff it can do. It's got this great game called Snake where you have to guide this line to the dots and—"

Marcus guffawed. "How retro."

"Maybe another time, Daisy. I really do have to finish my work. Professor Ramsbottom will open those heavy doors for you. He was just on his way out."

Marcus clenched his jaw. "Fine. See you anon, Madam Quinn. A true gentleman always knows when to take his leave." He clipped his feet together and walked in the opposite direction to the doors.

Susan quickly climbed out of her seat and sat on the table next to Daisy. "Do you think you've got five minutes to show me that game?"

Daisy giggled. "Okay, but I'll have to be quick. The smokers always meet about now at the bottom of the wall, and I want to get past before they arrive."

"Oh do they now? Right, you go. Get on your way." Susan tapped the side of her nose. "And thanks for the tip off. I knew you'd see sense. I'll finish my email and take a wander on down."

"No, Madam Quinn, I wasn't dropping them in it. I don't want them to think I'm a snitch."

Susan lifted the crutches and passed them to Daisy. "They won't know. I'll give you a ten minute head start."

"No, please, they'll know it's me."

"They won't. I'll wait a while."

Daisy shrugged. "They can be quite mean, I guess." She pushed up her glasses and grinned. "Fifteen minutes at least. I'm still pretty slow."

"They'll still be there?"

"They're always there on a Friday night."

Susan nodded. "I'll get back to my email then."

Daisy tucked the precious tablet under her arm. "But please don't get me into trouble, Madam Quinn. I'm not sure I could handle it if they got any worse."

"Oh Daisy, that's why they need pulling down a peg or two. You know how strict we are about smoking. Talk to me. Tell me what's going on."

"No, nothing really. I need to go. Timmy's waiting for me and he'll worry if I'm late." She paused. "But thank you for caring. Timmy cares too. I'm lucky to have you both looking out for me."

"Oh Daisy, I'm here whenever you need me."

"I know," said Daisy with a smile. "I need to get going."

Susan squeezed the little girl's shoulder. "You're sure?"

"I'm sure," said Daisy, hobbling away.

Susan returned to her seat and watched the little girl exit the library, before gasping and spinning around at the sound of a loud bang. "Marcus! What are you doing!?"

Marcus was frantically picking up a pile of books that had fallen from a trolley behind her. "Blasted thing. I didn't see it there."

"I thought you'd gone. Why are you loitering?"

"You won't let me use your internet. I'm finding my facts the traditional way." He brushed off his hands. "All done now though," he said, turning around and marching towards the exit.

Susan sighed to herself before quickly remembering where she'd been. She smiled and lifted her fingers back to her keyboard.

"**9.** Every time you ask me a new question because you want to get to know me more.

10. Every time you listen, I know you really care.

11. Every time you humour me, even though you know I'm being ridiculous.

12. Every time you talk about the future. Our future.

13. Every time you contact me, especially when it's unexpected.

14. Every time you—"

"Madam Quinn! Quick, it's Daisy!" Susan looked up at the double doors at Champagne Willington who had pushed her way into the library and was now panting for breath. "Quick! She needs help!"

Susan jumped up. "What? What is it?"

"Quickly, come on!" Champagne was waving her hand, guiding her teacher out onto the wide stone path that ran the length of the school. "Hurry! She's collapsed!"

"What? Where?" Susan was running alongside her student, past the main entrance and down the steep steps towards the long, winding drive. "Is she okay?"

"I don't know. She's in the soil patch!"

"What?" gasped Susan, trying to catch her breath, passing the tall stone wall that sheltered the school's bins. She glanced around, aware of some giggling girls. "Daisy!" she shouted, clambering across the small mound of soil. "Are you okay?"

Daisy was on her stomach, clutching her tablet into her chest. "My computer's okay, my computer's okay. At least my computer's okay."

Susan crouched down and wiped some of the soil from Daisy's face. "Oh dear, it looks like your glasses are cracked."

"But my computer's okay."

"What on earth happened? Can you move?" asked Susan, reaching out for the crutches.

Daisy sniffed. "I slipped. I just need some help to stand please."

Susan heard the giggles again. "Were you pushed? Did someone push you?"

"No, Madam Quinn. I just slipped."

"Daisy, you're knee deep in soil."

She shrugged. "I slipped."

Susan helped the little girl stand and looked over at the small group of girls hovering by the wall. "Come over here, right now," she demanded. "Did you girls see anything? Someone tell me what's gone on." Susan frowned. "Willamena, is that you? Willamena Edgington? What are you doing out here? I wouldn't have *you* down as a smoker."

Willamena cocked her head. "I don't smoke. Are you accusing me of smoking? I'll get my parents to complain if you are. Who's been telling you I smoke?" She sniggered. "Maybe Daisy's trying a new tan? The mud rub."

The group of girls giggled in unison.

"Enough, and for goodness sake, how many times do I need to tell you to wash that tattoo off your hand?" She pointed at the H8SKUWL biro-drawn logo scrawled into Willamena's skin. "Get inside all of you." She looked up at Champagne who was still panting. "What exactly did you see?"

"Nothing. Professor Ramsbottom told me."

"Told you what?"

"To grab you. I think he ran off for the nurse."

****

Marcus caught his breath and glanced around the library, plunging his hand into the breast pocket of his tweed jacket and pulling out the memory stick that had been burning a hole in there for the past few weeks. He swiped his finger over the mouse pad, thrilled that the computer hadn't gone to sleep. He scanned the page, drawn into the intensity of the emotional email. He stopped himself. This wasn't what he was here for. He minimised the page and clicked on the webcam tab, scrolling quickly to the camera roll instead.

Marcus groaned deeply, staring at the picture of the pork chop. *"Mon amie, mon amie, mon amie,"* he whispered, *"this, you forgot to delete."* He glanced around once more before plugging his memory stick into the computer and selecting all of the images.

CHAPTER TWENTY SEVEN

Susan jumped up onto the tall stool in her kitchen and switched on her Skype. Dealing with Daisy had taken an awful lot longer than she'd expected. The little girl couldn't see through her specs, so Susan had guided her to the medical room, expecting Danielle to be there with Marcus, but neither were anywhere to be seen, so she'd ended up sorting her out all by herself. Daisy had insisted she was fine, but after ten non-hypoallergenic wet wipes and three normal plasters, Susan had decided to call her mum and request that she come and collect her. Daisy had started to get upset until her tablet beeped with a message from Timmy telling her that he'd keep her company while she waited. Susan had realised then, that this was her cue to leave.

7.30 p.m., thought Susan, looking at the star-shaped clock hanging on the wall. 8.30 p.m. in Morzine. Jenna should still be around. She settled herself down on the stool and lifted her fingers to her laptop, clicking on Jenna's jpeg and waiting for the beeps to connect. "Hey, beautiful," she said as Jenna finally appeared in the screen.

"Hey, gorgeous," said Jenna, waving both hands and starting to laugh.

"What?"

"Why do I always feel the need to wave like a lunatic whenever I say hello on Skype or FaceTime? It's not like I used to meet you for breakfast in the morning at Sylvie's, frantically waving my hands as I said hello."

Susan laughed. "But when you get your training placement here I want you to wave in my face every time we pass in the staffroom."

Jenna shouted into the screen. "I'VE GOT IT!"

"What?" gasped Susan.

"The School Direct Programme! I've got an interview! You said if I get an interview it means I've got it! It means they want me!"

"When?! Wow!" Susan took hold of the sides of her laptop and shook the screen. "I'm so happy for you, Jenna! This is *amazing* news!"

Jenna was beaming from ear to ear, displaying her dimple in all its glory. "It gets better. It's Thursday!"

"Thursday? This Thursday?!" Susan was squealing like a little girl.

"THIS THURSDAY!"

"NO!"

"YES!"

Susan clasped her hand over her mouth and held back the tears. "I'm so proud of you, Jenna. So, so proud." She shook her head. "It's happening. It's really happening. You're going to work here. With me. We'll be together."

Jenna was nodding. "I hope so. The letter was here when I got back this afternoon." She lifted it up and flapped it in front of the screen. "It says they support my application and would like to meet for an official discussion and confirmation."

"So it doesn't even say the word interview?"

"No!"

"I told you! They know you! You're an old girl. Of course you were going to get it!"

"I'll fly over Wednesday and stay for the weekend!"

Susan couldn't hide her smile. "I love you so much, Jenna! This is amazing news." She clenched her fist and shook it in front of the screen. "I knew you'd get it! Didn't I tell you you'd get it?!"

"Shall we have a celebratory shag?" said Jenna with a smile.

Susan nodded. "Why not! But you'll have to be quick. I'm meeting Felicity, Jemima and Flavia soon."

"Flavia Simkins?"

"Yes, she came to Felicity's pamper night last week. We're all becoming rather good friends. I'm sure I told you."

Jenna grinned. "Susan, your social life's becoming so full that it's hard to keep up."

"Don't tease me."

"I'm not! I can't wait to get back over there and into the mix. We're going to grow such a great network of friends." She smiled and dropped her chin into her hands, sighing into the screen. "Susan, life's perfect. Isn't life perfect?"

Susan nodded. "It's sure looking that way, now do that kinky little dance of yours to seal the deal."

"You want me to talk again, like last time?"

Susan nodded. "Yes, but this time be more specific. Use words like *this Wednesday*, and *your apartment*." She paused. "And I like it when you use the words *harder, deeper, rougher.*"

"Your wish is my command," said Jenna, repositioning her laptop.

"Oh, hang on a minute, something's just come under the door." Susan climbed down from her stool. "I better check it." She spoke loudly as she walked out of view. "Last time it was a fire alarm notice." Susan picked up the large brown envelope and ran her finger under the tab, feeling the damp tackiness.

"What is it?" asked Jenna, smiling as Susan sat down.

"Not sure. But it's just been sealed. Let me check." She pulled out the pages of A4, instantly dropping the envelope in panic.

"What? What is it?"

Susan was frantically shaking her head. "NO!"

"What? Susan? What are you holding?"

Susan was shaking the print outs in her hand. "NO!"

"What? What is it?"

Susan gasped in horror and turned the first piece of paper towards her laptop screen.

"Hold it further back. I can't make it out."

Susan slammed her palm against the paper. "It's my pussy! MY PUSSY!"

"What? Susan, stop. It's not."

Susan was shaking the piece of paper at the screen. "It's my pussy! It's my fucking pussy! And these are my fucking tits!" She thrust the second piece of paper towards the webcam. "Oh look, and now a full frontal!" She shouted "OF ME!"

"Susan, stop it, calm down."

"Calm down? How can I calm down? Someone's just sent these under the door! I sent them to you, Jenna. TO YOU!"

"When? Today? In the post?"

"No!" Susan was flicking through the images. "Ages ago! The ones you said you deleted!"

"Which ones? When? I do delete. I delete everything."

Susan was gasping. "You obviously didn't! I sent these to YOU!"

"When?"

Susan widened her eyes. "Marcus! The ones he saw! We deleted the messages. You talked me through it. Remember? It's you! It must have come from you!"

"What? Susan, what are you talking about? I delete everything you send me. Always."

"Amber! She's seen your laptop, or your phone. You must have saved them." Susan climbed off the stool and started to pace. "She'll send them to the principal. She'll plaster them everywhere. She'll—"

"SUSAN!" Jenna was right in the screen. "STOP!"

Susan stood still and looked back at her laptop.

"Stop, re-live, and remember." Jenna was calmly beckoning Susan closer. "Look at me. Look at my eyes. Feel what we feel." Jenna smiled gently. "Know what we know." She paused for a moment. "You trust me. You know you trust me. So just listen. I delete every single picture. Every single message. Every single thing that's of a slightly risky nature. No matter how hot. I delete moments after viewing, or watching, or reading. I delete, Susan. This hasn't come from me."

Susan shook her head and continued to pace. "But—"

"Stop. Stand still. Calm down." Jenna was signalling Susan back over to the stool. "Sit down. We'll sort this out."

"How the HELL are we going to sort this out?! I've just had pictures of my pussy posted under the door!"

"Susan, sit down. Trust me, we'll sort this out."

Susan looked at the big brown eyes and paused. "How? Tell me how."

"Sit down, we'll talk through it." Jenna nodded encouragingly as Susan reluctantly climbed back onto the stool. "Show me each picture, one by one."

Susan held up the first image of her bra and cleavage. "One, my tits."

"Someone's tits."

"No, my tits."

"You can't see your head. They're just someone's tits."

Susan held up the next picture. "Two. My tits and my tummy."

"No, there's no head. That's just someone else's tits and someone else's tummy."

"Fine, three, a biology text book close up of my reproductive system."

"Looks like a pork chop to me, or maybe some beef curtains."

Susan tried not to smile. "Stop it. Four. A straight up shot of my legs, pussy and the bottom of my boobs."

"You straddled your laptop didn't you? I remember now. Up on your counter." Jenna shrugged. "But it's not you. It's just a mystery lady. A very hot mystery lady."

"Jenna, it's me!"

"But no one else knows it's you. Look at them. Look at them again. A faceless beauty."

"Whoever posted them knows it's me."

"Exactly," said Jenna.

"What?" Susan shook her head. "Marcus? No, never. How? When? We deleted them."

"Shit," gasped Jenna, suddenly clutching her mouth. "Your webcam. You took the pictures on your webcam. We deleted the Skype shots, but we didn't delete your webcam roll. Why would we? No one ever really uses their webcam camera roll."

Susan clicked on her keypad, minimising Jenna to the screen in the corner, quickly scrolling to her camera app. "It won't let me open it because I'm talking to you." She gasped. "But you're right though. I didn't think. I haven't used it since then. I've stuck with selfies. They'll still be on there. Someone's hacked in!"

"Occam's Razor."

"A hacking programme?"

"No!" said Jenna. "Occam's Razor. The simplest explanation is usually the right explanation. Who's had your laptop?"

"No one."

"You've never left it unattended, in easy reach of someone who knows what they're looking for? Someone who's threatened you before?"

Susan gasped replaying the events of the afternoon. "No! The little fucker!"

"The simplest explanation. Are there any notes? Anything else in the envelope?"

"I don't know. I dropped it. Let me look." Susan bent down and retrieved the package, shaking in anger as she drew out a small St Wilf's memory stick with a yellow post-it note attached. "Shit!" she shouted. "The fucking little shitter!"

"Let it all out, gorgeous, it'll help."

"The fucking little shit of a crappy pissing tosspot! He's left a note. It says: **Yours. All of it. No copies, I'm not that type of guy. Just be my witness on Thursday.**"

"Thursday?"

"His tribunal. He must have got his date." Susan jumped off the stool and shook her head, almost foaming at the mouth. "You're right. It's not me. He can stick this pile of shit right up his shitty little stinker!"

"I think pissing tosspot was better."

CHAPTER TWENTY EIGHT

Susan marched out of her living quarters and across the gravel path that linked her block to the next. She barged through the large double doors and headed towards the staff apartments, allowing her surge of anger to drive her forwards. She swerved around the corner and skidded to a stop as Marcus emerged from a door in front of her. "Take it," she said, stretching out the envelope and keeping her voice firm.

Marcus locked his door and started to walk.

"I said take it!"

"Quieten down, mon amie," hushed Marcus.

"Take it!" snapped Susan, keeping her voice loud.

"Not right now, I'm meeting Angel." He side stepped the onslaught and continued his journey. "We're off to salsa."

Susan spun around and chased after him. "You'll take these pictures and do whatever the hell you want with them. I'm talking to the tribunal and I'm telling them everything I know."

Marcus laughed. "No you're not. I'll show them. I'll show them all of these sordid little pictures." He stopped his walk and sneered. "I'll show everyone."

"I don't care."

"Yes you do," he said, turning around and marching away.

"Take them," shouted Susan, racing after him.

"Mon amie, have the weekend, you'll soon see sense." He rounded the corner and started the long walk down the oak covered corridor towards the grand entrance hall. "Oh look," he said, nodding at the new portrait of Ellen Cavanagh that was hanging from the wall, "there's a space to the right. Shall I pin you up there?"

"You are SO misguided. Thinking this, of all things, would make me vouch for your character."

Marcus stopped in front of Richard Jackson, 1993–2013. "You've left me no choice," he said with a sigh. "Look at you all selfless and principled. Fine. You might be selfless, but you're certainly not stupid."

"Pardon?"

He straightened the corner of his moustache and continued his walk. "Looks like it's my A-Game."

"What?" frowned Susan, matching his pace once more.

"My A-Game. Your girlfriend. She's next."

"Oh stop being so ridiculous, Marcus."

"Me! It's the two of you who bring this school into disrepute! What are they going to do? Ship me out on Thursday, bring her in on Friday?"

"Friday?"

"I've seen the schedule. It's a busy week. The final history and IT interviews on Thursday, not to mention the official appointment of the new vice principal. Then it's the School Direct and Trainee Teacher interviews on Friday."

"Friday?"

"You really think I'm going to let them approve her application if you've killed my character the night before?" He tapped his nose. "I'm a planner, my mon amie. I'm not worried."

Susan chased after him once more. "But you clearly *are* worried! Why on earth are you going to such lengths to try and secure me as a positive witness?"

"Because I'm innocent!" Marcus ran his fingers through his hair. "I've given my heart and soul to this school. I'm not silly, Susan, I know I'm not Mr Popular, but I try. I try really hard. Wouldn't you do anything you could to save your career from the warped mind of an aging despot?!"

"Dorothy?"

"Yes, Dorothy!"

"You're blowing this out of proportion."

"No, I'm not. This is *me* being called into question." Marcus snatched the envelope from Susan's hands. "Fine, don't help me. But just so you know, you're through as my friend."

"Oh, Marcus, please."

"No, I've got a life to live. What's left of it anyway. I'm off to salsa." Marcus stumbled over a loose lace and lost hold of the envelope, sending it skidding towards the tall trophy cabinet. He scooped down to pick it up and continued his walk.

Susan stopped in front of a very serious looking Elizabeth Warwick, 1854–1861, and watched as Marcus disappeared out of the double doors.

The voice was quiet. "Are you okay, Madam Quinn?"

Susan jumped. Little Daisy Button was sitting, hidden between two marble busts. "You're still here? Hasn't your mum arrived yet?"

Daisy shrugged. "She has to finish her shift. She clocks on and off. She won't be too long now." She grinned and tightened her grip on her tablet. "Plus I've got Snake."

"Can you see it okay?" asked Susan looking at the broken glasses.

"Yes, I just hold it really close."

"Shall I contact your mum and drive you home?"

Daisy shook her head. "Timmy's been here. He says he's coming back. Are you sure you're okay?"

Susan smiled. "Timmy's a good boy. You look after him."

Daisy giggled. "He's the one who looks after me. Remember I told you about that skate park he goes to on a Sunday? He's invited me. This weekend! I've got a boyfriend, Madam Quinn. I've actually got a boyfriend."

Susan crouched down next to the little girl. "Oh, Daisy, I'm so happy for you."

"You're my favourite teacher; you know that don't you?"

"That's kind."

"No, you are, and I'll help you if I can."

"With what?"

Daisy shrugged. "With whatever's going on."

Susan smiled. "You're a real little hero, Miss Daisy Button."

"*I will be*," whispered Daisy as she watched her teacher walk away.

****

Daisy waited for Madam Quinn to disappear back down the corridor before lifting herself onto her crutches. She'd seen it drop. She knew what it was. She hobbled over to the large trophy cabinet and bent down to retrieve the small St Wilfred's memory stick. They were only ten pounds from the school shop, but ten pounds was too much. She'd just stick it in, she thought, and see what it does. Her tablet might make a new noise when it was detected, or maybe even flash up with an exciting new message. She smiled to herself, thrilled at the thought, then nodded in decision. But she'd be the hero. She'd hand it back. She'd hand it back and save the day. It was obviously important to both Madam Quinn and Professor Ramsbottom as they were clinging onto the brown envelope for dear life. Maybe it was full of coursework marks, or early exam results, thought Daisy, hobbling back to her hiding place.

Daisy brought the tablet close to her face and pushed the stick into the port. She watched with excitement as a multi-coloured circle started to spin. Suddenly there was a new box and some photos. She tapped on one of the jpegs and tilted her head, unable to make anything out in the picture apart from the big brown Moroccan pendant lamp hanging from the ceiling that Madam Quinn had done an assembly on once. She rubbed her glasses and stared even closer, gasping as the picture suddenly came into focus. She closed it down quickly but another flashed up of the lovely butterfly blouse that Madam Quinn always wore on a Wednesday, but it was open and there was a bra and—

"Daisy Button! You little thief!" Marcus Ramsbottom was back in the entrance hall, flapping the envelope. "I've just seen you plug that stick in. Where did you find it?"

Daisy pulled out the small blue device and held it tightly in her hand. "I didn't steal it. I found it on the floor over there." She pointed towards the trophy cabinet. "I was going to hand it in."

Marcus stepped closer and prised the stick from her palm. "You were stealing it."

"I wasn't!"

"It probably wouldn't even work in that cheap tablet of yours."

Daisy tried to get eye contact as best she could through her broken spectacles. "It worked."

"What?"

Daisy Button stood up and peered even closer at her teacher. "It worked."

"Stop it, Daisy. You look like that scary toon from the *Who Framed Roger Rabbit* film. What was he called? Judge Doom."

Daisy hadn't got a clue what he was talking about but knew he felt threatened. "It worked," she said again.

Marcus shoved the memory stick into the breast pocket of his well-worn tweed jacket and tapped it securely. "Fine, you've had a sneak peek. You were bound to see them eventually."

"You're going to show people? Those pictures of Madam Quinn?"

Marcus sneered. "Your favourite teacher isn't as perfect as everyone thinks."

"I'll tell her," gasped Daisy.

"She knows. Didn't you see her give me the envelope back?" Marcus tapped his breast pocket once more. "It's only a matter of time," he said, turning around and walking away. "Only a matter of time."

Daisy grabbed her crutches and tried to hobble after him, but gave up at the upholstered benches next to the main oak doors, realising he was too far away. She sat down and caught her breath, rubbing her glasses as a blurry figure stepped out of Principal Cavanagh's office.

"So you did snitch on us then," said the voice. "I knew you would."

"What? No!"

"Yes, you did. I've just been suspended for smoking, and so have Henrietta and Gloria. You know we'll get you back for this."

Daisy squinted as the person came into focus. "Is that why you pushed me? Because you thought I would tell?"

"You did tell. We got caught twenty minutes ago."

"I didn't tell. I wouldn't tell."

"Well someone did and you always walk past us."

"Is that why you pushed me? To warn me?"

Willamena Edgington shrugged. "I'm glad I got caught. The man in my life hates it when I smoke."

Daisy quickly tapped her tablet, keen to get Willamena on side. "I've got a man in my life too. I was walking to meet him. I didn't have time to go and tell. I've been in the medical room. Here," she said, proudly holding up the picture of her and Timmy. "He's my boyfriend now. He's just asked me out."

"Ha!" laughed Willamena, "I'm sixteen, as if I'm going to be interested in Justin Bieber and his bag of flour."

Daisy tapped to another one. "He really likes me. I'm a cool girl now. I've got my man, I've got a tan, and I wouldn't snitch."

Willamena sat down on the bench. "What are you both? Eleven?"

Daisy nodded. "He's taking me to the skate park on Sunday. There are loads of smokers there. I don't mind them at all. I'll even support my man around the smokers. I wouldn't snitch."

Willamena laughed and swiped the screen on her own phone. "He's not a man."

Daisy watched as Willamena scrolled to her Twitter app and clicked on the private message button.

"*This* is a man."

Daisy looked at the jpeg of the pale torso, complete with orange hairs. "Gross."

"No it's not. It's a real man." Willamena wiggled the phone. "You don't get sent selfies from real men, do you?"

Daisy glanced at the image once more as a vision of the ski trip and accidental door opening flashed into her mind. "Is that—"

"I bet you don't even have Twitter. Facebook's so unfashionable nowadays."

Daisy studied the large biro-drawn tattoo that was a constant on the back of Willamena's hand. It always said: H8SKUWL, and was decorated today with lightning bolts and what looked like a badly sketched skull. "I might get it." She paused. "Do I have to pay?"

Willamena snorted. "It's just your email address, divvy."

CHAPTER TWENTY NINE

Daisy sat down on her bed in her badly decorated bedroom. She had a plan. She'd be the hero. She'd use her super computer to save the day. She reached backwards to the moneybox that was gathering dust on the window ledge and pulled out the lonely ten pound note she had received from her Grandma at Christmas. She had been saving it for her mum's birthday next month, but *this* was definitely more important. *This* was an emergency. She folded it into a small square and reached down to the floor for her schoolbag, tucking the note safely into the pocket at the back and closing the zip. She would go to the school shop first thing Monday morning. She would buy a blue one. She would make the swap. Thursday. Period 3. That was her chance.

Daisy looked once more at the jpegs she had saved into her new special folder, named: **MissionHero**. How silly of Willamena, she thought, to use such an obvious password. A password right there, for everyone to see.

CHAPTER THIRTY

Susan moved her hand under the table and stroked the leg that was resting against her own. "It's so good to have you back," she said, smiling widely, and absorbing the peaceful atmosphere in the Black Bear pub.

"How many times are you going to say it?" laughed Jenna, finding the hand with her own and squeezing it right back.

"At least a hundred." Susan lifted her glass of sparkling white wine and held it out as a toast to her girlfriend. "And I'm going to cheers us at least a hundred times too."

Jenna chinked her drink against Susan's. "Okay, but let me do it this time." She smiled. "To us. To our future. To a taste of our life to come."

Susan chinked back and took another sip. "You're right. This is what it'll be like: Random Wednesday evening meals in the pub, impromptu shopping trips after school."

"It was you who said that my suit was too short. I was all set to go."

"It was, but now you'll look sensational."

Jenna laughed. "I can't believe you got me to try on that woollen skirt and jacket combo from Cotton Traders."

"It was top quality."

"I looked fifty five!"

Susan smiled. "Hobbs to the rescue. Tomorrow you'll be smart, sophisticated, and sexily hot, in a professional power-trip sort of way."

"Should I do my hair and make-up?"

"Of course you should, and we're getting rid of that three-in-one shampoo, conditioner and body wash of yours. We'll make sure our morning routines are never rushed."

"Trust me. I'm keeping you busy in bed. They'll be rushed." She grinned. "What are our chances of getting the apartment in the larger living quarters?"

Susan shrugged. "I've asked provisionally, but I think it's best to wait until we get your final confirmation tomorrow. I'll wait for you outside Ellen's office. We'll go straight up and see Afia from accommodation."

Jenna smiled. "There's no doubt in your mind is there?"

"That they'll offer you the programme? No, no doubt at all." Susan paused. "Well, maybe there was a slight niggle of a doubt at the back end of last week, but Marcus would have played his hand by now. His tribunal's at 6.00 p.m. tomorrow. You did check with Hugo though didn't you?"

Jenna nodded. "Hugo, Lisa, Amber. Crikey, I sent an email around the whole of Club Ski telling everyone to delete everything. Juvenile Jenna James is no more. But that prick of a pretend professor, Marcus Rat-Arse Ramsbottom—"

"Did I just hear you mention my mister smoochy pants?" giggled Angel, tottering over with two large plates of food. "If we marry I'll become a princess."

"Pardon?" said Susan, leaning back slightly as the steaming roast dinner was presented in front of her.

"What's the female equivalent of a professor? Is it a princess, or a lady? Or what's that other one? A duchess. That's it. Which one will I get?"

Jenna moved her glass to make room for her plate. "When you marry Professor Ramsbottom?"

Susan cut in, not wanting Jenna to make a smart remark. "I think the female version of a professor is just a professor."

Angel fanned her face. "Could you imagine? Professor Angel DeLorias."

"Going well, is it?" asked Jenna, trying not to smile.

Angel took a breath and perched herself down on the seat next to them. "Strong but silent is my mister smoochy pants." She paused. "Sometimes, if I'm honest though, I'm not quite sure where we stand."

"What do you mean?" asked Susan, lifting her cutlery and signalling for Jenna to start.

"Oh you know, I don't want to talk out of turn, but it's always on his terms. I guess I sometimes feel like a bit of a show pony. Like he's only interested in me when other people are around."

Susan smiled. "You're not a show pony, Angel. You're a thoroughbred prize winner."

"Oh honey, you really think?"

"I really think."

Angel lowered her voice. "Well if it doesn't work out with him I've got my mister sweetie pie." She tilted her head. "At the bar. Doctor. Consultant I think. What's the female version of a consultant? A sultan? Would I be a sultan?"

"Yes, I think you would," said Jenna, cutting into a piece of pork.

"Oh ladies, you're lovely. I'll leave you in peace." She stood up and straightened her pink neon skirt. "One last thing." She pointed at the jukebox. "Those girls. They say they're eighteen. They're yours aren't they?"

Susan leaned to the side and spotted Champagne Willington and Priggy Bunton-Chatsworth hovering by the jukebox. "Yes. They're eighteen."

"Always good to check. I wouldn't want to lose us our licence. What would my mister cuddle tums say?"

Jenna frowned. "Cuddle tums?"

"Owner. He wants to add a huge coffee machine to the bar. Says it'll make me a barrister, but I've never liked law." Angel shrugged. "C'est la vie." She smiled. "My mister smoochy pants taught me that. He really is a good guy you know."

Jenna struggled to swallow. "He's—"

"We know," said Susan. "We'll tell him to call."

"Thank you, honey. Enjoy your meals, and slip me the nod if you want extra gravy," said Angel, making her way back to the bar.

"Misguided," said Jenna, shaking her head.

"But so is he," said Susan, "and I do feel really rather sorry for him. What if—"

"Stop, don't start. Tonight's about us, our future, the future that Professor Up-My-Own-Arsey Pants won't be part of. What time's his thing again?"

"Six p.m, in the meeting room."

"Can I come?"

"I doubt it. But we've got that staff meeting at four, which you'll be part of."

"*If* I get the placement."

"*When* you get the placement. They'll introduce you, and I think they're making the final appointments tomorrow for three other roles as well, so they'll introduce those people too."

Jenna nodded. "I looked on the board. It's the new vice principal, the new IT teacher, and what was the other one?"

"History," said Susan, slicing into her beans.

"How long will it last?"

"Not too long. Ellen will introduce you all, get you to say hello, embarrass you by reciting your credentials. We had one last week when they appointed the new art teacher. It's all very exciting and completely over the top, but Ellen says a warm welcome's the perfect way to start something special."

"She seems really good."

"She is, she's great." Susan tutted at the presence behind her. "I know you're hovering back there."

Champagne and Priggy sheepishly stepped into view. "We've tried to give you your space, but we can't! She's back! She's here! We're so excited!"

Jenna shoved along in her seat. "Come on then, come join us. Tell us all of your news."

The girls glanced at Susan.

"Go on," said Susan with a smile, "I've got some catching up to do too. Now, remind me again. Is it Edward and Bella or Mischa and Phats?"

Priggy laughed hysterically.

"It wasn't that funny, Priggs," said Champagne, sitting down and lifting her arm up to her teacher's shoulder, "but I'm glad you're back, Susie. That Madam Quinn's been a right royal—"

"Champs!" Priggy kicked her friend under the table.

Susan smiled. "It's fine. She's right. It's been a difficult time. But things are certainly looking up."

"US TOO!" shouted Priggy. "WE GOT INTO MANCHESTER!"

Champagne licked her finger and darted it through the air. "I'll be there with bad boy Phats!"

Priggy tried to do the same thing. "And I'll be there with munch me Mischa!"

Everyone at the table moaned. "Priggy!"

"What?"

Jenna smiled. "You'll have a brilliant time. You should both be really proud of yourselves."

"We have to get the grades first," said Champagne, starting to pout.

"A-grade students," said Susan.

Priggy's eyes were wide. "You think?"

"I know."

"Oh Susie, you're so sweet." Champagne reached out her arms. "I love this version of you. Come on, ski circle cuddle everyone."

Priggy edged even closer to her teacher, thrilled by the giddiness of their celebrations. "Ski circle snuggle."

Champagne rolled her eyes. "I said cuddle, Priggy, not snuggle."

Priggy removed her hand from Susan's waist. "Oh, sorry, Champs. Sorry, Madam Quinn." She paused, looking at the table full of food. "Come on, let's leave them to it. We just wanted to say hi, and bye, and that we'll miss you."

Champagne shrugged. "Yeah we're gutted we won't be here next year. You're going to be amazing Jenna, and you're great too, Susie."

"It's Madam Qui ..." Susan paused. "Thank you, Champagne."

Priggy nodded. "And you'll never guess what? Our courses can be linked to the teacher training programme after two years if we want."

"God help us," laughed Jenna.

Champagne flicked her hair. "Hey, if they take you, they're bound to take us."

"Oi, you cheeky beggar."

"Seriously," said Champagne, "good luck for tomorrow. You're our role model, Jenna." She paused. "Priggy and I think you're fab."

"And you too, Madam Quinn," added Priggy far too quickly.

Susan smiled and lifted her glass. "To tomorrow."

"To tomorrow," they cheered.

CHAPTER THIRTY ONE

Susan kept her eyes on the large oak door. It was 3.45 p.m. What was taking so long? Ellen Cavanagh was needed in the staffroom at 4.00 p.m. to introduce and welcome today's newly appointed teachers, so why weren't they coming out? What was the delay? Susan checked her watch and glanced around the imposing entrance hall. Had she missed them? No, of course she hadn't. She had been sitting there the whole time, eyes glued to the door. She took a deep breath and bit the inside of her lip, carefully trying to think it through. Jenna had entered the principal's office an hour ago, looking every bit the professional. But why wasn't she out? How long could it possibly take to confirm a training placement? Had Marcus got in there first? Had he shown Ellen something to make her reconsider? Had he smeared Jenna's name. Had he sabotaged—

"I got it!" gasped Jenna, in an excitedly hushed voice, racing her way across the large wooden expanse towards the upholstered benches. "I got it!" She made a fist in the air, quickly glancing back to check she'd closed the door behind her. She had, so she made a double fist in the air and jumped up and down. "I got it!"

Susan dashed up from her seat and scurried towards her girlfriend. "You got it?"

"I got it!" said Jenna, throwing her arms around Susan's back and holding her tightly. "I got it!"

Susan breathed in Jenna's sweet smell, trying her best to control her emotions. "I'm so proud of you," she whispered. "So, so proud."

Jenna let her lips brush against Susan's ear, stealing a quick kiss, before stepping backwards and straightening her suit. "Principal Cavanagh said she'd be out in a minute. She's walking me to the staffroom. She says *all* of the staff will be there. I'm getting introduced! As a professional! Me! Jenna James! A trainee teacher!" She straightened her suit once more and tried to control her giggles. "That's what took so long. She'd lost my list of credentials. A mix up with the day of my interview or something. She says it's been hectic what with all the other appointments this week. But anyway, it's done. She's putting a picture of me on the PowerPoint with the title: Jenna James, School Direct Trainee Teacher – Drama. She even took a new photo of me. It was hilarious because she couldn't get the camera working, but anyway. Can you imagine? Little old me, entering the staffroom with the principal of St Wilfred's." Jenna laughed. "This is all so exciting."

"Ooo, I better go ahead then," giggled Susan, "and don't worry, Afia from accommodation's bound to be there. We can catch up with her afterwards. Hang on, no, there she is now!" Susan spotted the small woman marching past the marble busts. "Afia! Afia! A quick second!"

The woman stopped her walk and waved in response.

"I'll walk down with her now. I'm so proud of you," said Susan, "so proud!" She smiled and gave Jenna's shoulders a final squeeze. "I'll see you in there."

Ellen Cavanagh emerged from her office with her hand outstretched, signalling towards the long oak corridor. "Madam James, after you."

Jenna tried to keep a straight face. "Thank you, Principal Cavanagh."

Susan watched as her girlfriend walked off, looking every inch the perfect professional. "Afia," she said again, scurrying quickly towards the marble busts, "Jenna's got it! She's in! She's starting in September!"

The small lady smiled. "And you want first dibs on the apartment in the larger living quarters?"

"If you think that's okay?"

Afia nudged Susan's arm. "Of course it's okay. First come first served," she said with a giggle. "But I don't think those two luscious ladies in the staffroom will be best pleased."

"What ladies?"

Afia started to walk. "I'll show you," she said, smiling conspiratorially. "It's unofficial gossip, but apparently there's been a young couple appointed. Looks to die for. Moving down here from—"

"Mon amie, mon amie, un momento!" Marcus Ramsbottom was marching through the main entrance.

"I'll see you in there," said Afia.

"Save me a seat, and thank you, you're a star."

Afia shrugged. "Jenna's great. I think you're *both* really great together. I'm thrilled that she's staying."

Marcus sighed as the lady walked away. "Staying? Oh little does she know."

"Pardon?"

"I've taken it to the wire. I've given you ample opportunity to see sense. I've given you space. I've kept my distance. But no. There's been no word from you. You haven't come to find me. You haven't asked how things are." He sighed. "So you leave me no choice. Two hours from now we'll be at my tribunal, or tittle tattle talk through as I prefer to call it. Be kind. Be positive, and show me support." He licked the corners of his moustache in achievement. "Or I'll take this to Principal Cavanagh tonight." He pulled the blue memory stick from the breast pocket of his tweed jacket.

Susan rolled her eyes. "I don't care if you show people my selfies."

"Oh no, no, no, no, no, my mon amie. These aren't just your selfies. These are your selfies, *and* some crystal clear tequila tit shots. Jenna James bare chested. Liquor lashing down her breast. Ladies at her knee licking their lips." He moaned. "Such a shame I can't keep them to myself." He shrugged. "But I can't, can I? We wouldn't want someone like that working at a prestigious establishment like this." He shrugged again. "Her interview's tomorrow. Such a shame if someone sees them tonight."

Susan laughed. "Oh you totally misguided twat of a tosspot!"

"Mon amie!"

Susan laughed again. "She's got the placement! It's just been confirmed!" She nodded towards the principal portraits and the slow stream of teachers heading down the long corridor. "The staff meeting that everyone's going to, she's already there." Susan paused. "With her new best friend, Principal Cavanagh. You know how charismatic Jenna is. Their interview ran over. They were having such a great laugh. She's getting officially introduced and welcomed. You're too late, Marcus. You're just too late."

"Today? No! When? I've been saving these pictures!"

Susan shrugged her shoulders and started to walk. "What does it matter? *She'll* be here in September, but I doubt we can say the same about *you*."

"How dare you!" gasped Marcus. "And who's we?!" He flapped his arms and started to fume. "I'll show you! I'll show all of you!" Marcus clutched the blue stick and marched straight past her, shouting louder as he picked up speed. "You people are wrong! You're all so wrong! I'll show you who's right! Questioning my integrity whilst you employ a woman like that!" Marcus waved the stick in the air and started to run. "I'm a teacher! She's nothing! She's nobody! I won't let this happen!"

"Marcus, stop, wait!" Susan upped her pace, stumbling slightly as she passed the peering portrait of Edward Sears, 1922–1929.

"You can't stop me now! I'm a man on a mission! A saviour of the school! A paragon of—" Marcus jumped to the left as Martha Adams and Mary Llewellyn sped round the corner, narrowly missing him with their mobility scooter.

"Madam Quinn," shouted Martha, "there's something wrong with the motor! Stand to the side!" She was waving her hand and frowning in panic. "Wait, no, whoa!"

Susan watched as the two old ladies wobbled around on the red machine, swerving towards the trophy cabinet. "Use the brakes!" she shouted.

"We know it shakes!" yelled Mary.

Susan shouted louder as the scooter sped closer. "The switch! Turn off the switch!"

"Don't call her a bitch!" said Mary. "She's not trying to hit you! She's—"

"Ahhhh!" came the scream as the scooter stopped suddenly, sending both old ladies skidding down onto their knees.

Susan raced to their side. "Are you okay? What can I do?"

"You and your bloody tinkering, Mary." Martha Adams was dusting off her skirt. "I wish you'd just leave it alone."

"You've broken a bone?" Mary Llewellyn pulled herself up from the floor.

Susan glanced down the corridor. "I'm sorry, I've got to go."

Martha tutted. "You can't leave an old woman lying on the floor! Pass me the port!"

Susan felt a surge of panic. "Sorry, no, of course not, hang on."

****

Ellen Cavanagh was holding court in front of her staff, smiling with warmth and exuding her expertise as a people person, aware of the importance of good first impressions. She clicked on the PowerPoint and nodded. The current staff had to respect the new staff, and the new staff had to feel welcomed. "So, first I'd like to introduce

Nicola Stevens who'll be joining us in the IT Department." Ellen waited for the clapping to die down, knowing that her fancy 'Faces & Facts' PowerPoint presentation achieved both aims. The staff nodded as she pointed out Nicola's previous achievements, and Nicola blushed at their cheers.

****

"Anything else I can do?" asked Susan, quickly pushing the machine up against the wall.

"Yes a real hullabaloo!" nodded Mary, taking a swig from the hip flask.

"No, sorry, listen, I need to get to the staffroom." She glanced down the corridor. "I *really* need to get to the staffroom."

****

Ellen ended her clapping and signalled for Jenna to stand. "And now we have a somewhat familiar face amongst us all. Some of you taught her and some of you were teaching before she was born."

Dorothy Brown's muttering was drowned out with the laughter.

"Let's welcome Jenna James back to St Wilfred's. She's joining us on the School Direct programme and will be an active member of the Arts Faculty. She'll complete her teacher training onsite, and in just over a year she'll be a fully-fledged drama teacher."

"Hopefully," said Jenna with a smile.

"Most certainly," said Ellen, clicking onto the PowerPoint presentation. "Jenna not only excelled as a student here at St Wilfred's, gaining straight As in her exams, but she went on to achieve a first class degree from Durham."

****

Susan raced down the corridor and swerved around the corner, narrowly missing Daisy Button and her crutches.

"Madam Quinn—"

"Not now, Daisy!" shouted Susan, continuing her run.

"But—"

"Not now!"

****

Marcus heard the sound of the shoes fast approaching. "You should have stuck with me, sweetheart," he shouted, as Susan came into view.

"Marcus, don't!"

Marcus shrugged his shoulders as he pushed through the staffroom door. Jenna was standing at the front with Ellen. "Well isn't this nice," he shouted, interrupting the applause.

"Take a seat please, Professor Ramsbottom." Ellen was pointing to the chairs that were vacant in the corner of the room.

"Oh no, sorry, I need centre stage for this." He edged his way to the front and stopped next to the laptop that was sitting on top of the IT trolley. "Connected to the big screen, isn't it?"

****

Susan skidded to a stop at the staffroom door, clutching the handle and pushing the door ajar. She gasped. He was at the front. He was plugging it in. She stood still, unable to enter the room.

****

"Excuse me please, Professor Ramsbottom, I'd like you to take a seat." Ellen glanced at the new vice principal who was sitting silently, observing proceedings. "Now please."

"Un momento, my inexperienced little line manager."

"Excuse me?"

"Everyone makes mistakes. It's human nature. No one will blame you. You can rectify this very quickly."

A couple of members of staff started to mutter.

Ellen barked. "Sit down, Professor."

"Not even willing to address her own error." He looked at the room. "I think that speaks volumes about our new principal."

"Wrap it up, Ramsbottom," shouted Mel Copeland from the back of the room.

"Please, everyone. I've got two more introductions to make. Jenna, take a seat, and thank you very much, you'll be a wonderful addition to the school. Marcus, this is the last time I'll ask you. Take a seat, please."

Marcus Ramsbottom pushed the blue stick into the laptop, quickly clicking on play. "Our new arrival," he shouted, sticking his thumb up to the screen behind him. "What a perfect appointment!"

****

Susan released her grip on the handle and let the door close, turning around and crouching down against the cold corridor wall. She couldn't watch it. She couldn't bear to see their dreams shattered. She took a deep breath and sighed at her own stupidity. If only she'd listened. If only she'd done what he wanted.

****

The room fell silent.

"Thank you VERY much!" he wailed, bursting with glee. "Do we really want someone like this teaching our children? Do we really want the reputation of St Wilfred's tarnished by titillation?"

"Turn it off," gasped Ellen.

Marcus continued to address the room. "Oh no, no, no, there's more to come. You wait till you see our very own Madam—" Marcus stopped as the sniggers got louder. "You think this is funny? You think we should allow this kind of behaviour in our school?"

"Flex 'em, cowboy!" shouted Mel Copeland.

Afia from accommodation giggled loudly. "Tense that torso!"

"Ha! The ginger giant!" shouted Danielle Watts. "I've seen bigger biceps on my budgie!"

Marcus span around. His face was filling the screen. He was flexing his muscles and pulling a pout. "Wait! What? No!"

"Mel, a hand please," said Ellen to the tall PE teacher who was laughing loudly at the back of the room.

Mel Copeland stood up and pounded her way to the front. "You want him out?"

Marcus was foaming at the mouth. "This isn't right! I've been set up!"

Ellen looked once more at the newly appointed vice principal. "I'm terribly sorry, there's a tribunal tonight. It's an ongoing issue which I assure you will be resolved by September."

Dorothy Brown stood up and punched her fist into the air. "My final triumph! I knew I was right! I can retire now with relish!"

****

Susan tilted her head at the cheering. What on earth was going on? She opened her eyes and stood back up, ready to push through the door, stopped by the gentle tugging on her sleeve.

"This is for you, Madam Quinn." Daisy Button held up the small St Wilfred's memory stick.

Susan looked down at the wide eyes. "Daisy, what's this?"

"A thank you."

Susan spotted a trace of colour in the little girl's cheeks. "For what?"

"For everything." Her smile was wide. "You've been my hero; now I hope I'll be yours."

****

Ellen watched the kerfuffle at the back of the room. Marcus wasn't going quietly. "I really am sorry," she said to her staff. "Right, who am I doing next?" She fumbled with the laptop, trying to find the right screen.

"I've been set up!" came the final shout from Marcus, as Mel Copeland opted for the fireman's lift.

Ellen was stuttering and stammering. "Who was I doing next? Umm, let me see, shall we go to history? Yes, history and Freya, no." She quickly clicked through more screens. "Sorry, no, we're doing the vice principal next. Right," she said, standing up taller as the correct face finally flashed up. "Let's show a warm welcome the new vice principal of St Wilfred's."

"SET UP I TELL YOU!" shouted Marcus, managing to barge his way back into the room.

Ellen flared up with colour, shouting over the noise. "Miss Katherine Spicer."

Kat took a slow breath and twisted in her seat, whispering to her girlfriend with worry. "What sort of place is this?"

Freya's green eyes twinkled. "I don't know, but it sure looks like fun to me."

THE END

About the author:

Kiki Archer is a UK-based lesbian fiction novelist and winner of the Ultimate Planet's Independent Author of the Year Award 2013.

Her debut novel, the best-selling **"But She is My Student,"** won the UK's 2012 SoSoGay Best Book Award.

Its sequel, **"Instigations,"** took just 12 hours from its release to reach the top of the UK lesbian fiction chart.

Kiki also topped the lesbian fiction charts in 2013 with her best-selling third novel, **"Binding Devotion,"** which was a 2013 Rainbow Awards finalist.

"One Foot Onto The Ice" has been her most successful novel to date, breaking into the American contemporary fiction top 100 as well as achieving the US and UK lesbian fiction number one.

Novels by Kiki Archer:

BUT SHE IS MY STUDENT - March 2012

INSTIGATIONS - August 2012

BINDING DEVOTION - February 2013

ONE FOOT ONTO THE ICE - September 2013

WHEN YOU KNOW - April 2014

Connect with Kiki:

www.kikiarcher.com
Twitter: @kikiarcherbooks
www.facebook.com/kiki.archer

8990766R00129

Printed in Great Britain
by Amazon.co.uk, Ltd.,
Marston Gate.